"It's not what happ,
you in life which
It's how you respon
makes all the difference."

CW00701101

100 DAYS TO
MENTAL RESILIENCE

By John Dabrowski

Best Wishes

First published in 2020 by Solopreneur Publishing, West Yorkshire U.K

The Solopreneur Publishing Company Ltd focuses on the needs of each author client. This book has been published through their 'Solopreneur Self-Publishing (SSP)' brand that enables authors to have complete control over their finished book whilst utilising the expert advice and services usually reserved for traditionally published print, in order to produce an attractive, engaging, quality product. Please note, however, that final editorial decisions, clearances, and approval rests with the author.

ISBN 978-1-9164415-9-0
Printed in the U.K.

Photo: John Dabrowski back cover provided by Julie Dabrowski.

PLEASE NOTE:
There are many stories used within this book to illustrate the 'Thought for Today' created. I would like to thank personally 'Word for Today' (written by Bob and Debby Gass and published by UCB) for providing so much inspiration throughout the last ten years, along with many of the stories. I have also taken inspiration from various website searches and newspaper articles. I thank all the contributions, but as the stories have been collated over ten years, I apologise if I have been unable to establish every source. If anyone knows the exact source of any of the stories used, please email me at – john@jdmindcoach.com, and I will amend for the next print run.

Many thanks … John Dabrowski

Dedicated to ....

My dear sister Christina who passed away on the 27th April 2018. She is missed by all my family and her friends. I have very fond memories of the great times we shared. She was instrumental in helping me write my first book, and I know that she would have been involved in this book if she were still with us.

"Three questions to ask at the end of our lives …

Did we live?
Did we make a difference?
Did we matter?"

Brendon Buchard

ACKNOWLEDGEMENTS

I would like to thank Michael Dobson and Paula Chantler-Dobson for helping to put this book together; it has been great to work with you both. Michael, your work with the cover design and some of the content of the book has been invaluable, and Paula, your proofreading skills have been amazing.

One person who has been with me throughout my life journey is my precious 96-year-old mum Janina. She is a wonderful person who I am immensely proud to call my mum. She has supported me in all my ups and downs and has never judged me. She has simply been there to pick me up when I needed it and has celebrated my victories with me.

Finally, a very special thank you to my dear wife, Julie, who is the light of my life. We have been married for 5 years, she is my rock, and we are just as much in love now as we were when we first met. She is a great influence on my business, and she encouraged me to write this book supporting me throughout the journey. She also has a hidden talent for photography and took the photo of me, which sits proudly on the back cover.

100 STORIES TO DEVELOP MENTAL RESILIENCE

18   It's not what happens – Fire in Her Heart
21   The Power of persistence – Tyler Perry
24   An encouraging word – Emily Blunt
27   The right attitude – What am I?
30   Dealing with rejection – Sylvester Stallone
33   Amazing determination – Grandma Cha Soon
36   Mental movies – Jim Carrey
39   Broke but he had a dream – Colonel Sanders KFC
42   The damage caused by anger – Nails in the Fence
45   Broken relationships – The Keys in the Book
49   A kind gesture – The Ice Cream Sundae
52   It's all about perspective – Car Crash in Asda
55   The power of gratitude – Blind Couple on a Train
58   A Remarkable Story – Helen Keller
61   Rest and plan – The Lumberjack Story
64   The futility of fame and fortune – Muhammad Ali
67   Encouragement – Stand and Deliver
70   Negative anchor – A Trip to Poland
73   Setting goals – Wales and England Football
76   The birth of a superstar – Olympian Adam Peaty
80   Not defined by your past – The Pursuit of Happiness
83   A national hero – Karoly Takacs
86   Belief system – Elephant Rope
89   Commitment – Playing Basketball for England
92   Self-talk – The Boy in the Fire
95   He lost his legs – Hugh Herr Frostbite
98   From broke to billionaire – WhatsApp Story
101   How we respond – Potato Eggs and Coffee Beans
104   Planning for failure? – The Ant and the Grasshopper
107   What you do makes a difference – Keeper of the Spring
111   A positive from a negative – 3M Post it Notes

114 Adversity is the grindstone of life – Abraham Lincoln
117 Dreams do come true – In Dubai at Last
120 The power of caring – He was Prepared to Die
123 The importance of love – The Gold Box
126 The power of Integrity – Davis Love US PGA
129 An impossible achievement – Brooklyn Bridge
132 It's how you finish – Waterstones Book Signing
135 Never give up – Bear Grylls
138 A random act of kindness – Nat King Cole
142 Learn to bounce back – Walt Disney
145 It's how you respond – Paganini and the Cruise
148 This is why I do what I do – A story of Confidence
151 Visualise Your Future - Arnold Schwarzenegger
154 It's how you finish – The House Builder
157 From rags to riches – Andrew Carnegie
160 Mindfulness – If I Had my Life Over
163 Dream board – Waterstones Book Launch
166 The whole world came together – The Picture Puzzle
169 Speak positive words – The Blind Man in Hospital
173 An act of kindness – The Two Apples
176 Momentum is the key – From Good to Great
179 Reap what you sow – Shania Twain Sacrifice
182 Shake off your problems – The Donkey in the Well
185 Patience for the long haul – Chinese Bamboo
188 Plan your time carefully – A Special Bank Account
191 The obstacle in your path – The Bag of Gold
194 Make a difference – The Starfish
197 Helping equals happiness – The 5-star Chef
200 Purpose and Passion – Suicide Jumper Survives
204 Your belief system – The Shark Experiment
207 You take your attitude with you – Wise Old Man
210 The power of gratitude – Be Thankful
214 The small details – The Bag of Marbles
217 What describes you – The Monk in the Monastery
220 You have amazing potential – The Two Camels
223 Encouragement – From Janitor to Principal

226 Things aren't always what they seem – Two Angels
229 The world is your oyster – Magic Johnson
232 Perception is reality – The Four Seasons of Life
236 Dreams do come true – 10-Year-Old's Dream Board
239 Integrity for life – The USA Open Bobby Jones
242 Overcome fear – Forget Yesterday and Tomorrow
245 A dog's purpose – Belker the Dog
248 Stop and smell the roses – If a dog was a teacher
251 A positive inner voice – My Wedding Day
254 Preparation for your future – Daniel Webster
257 A good attitude opens the door – Stanford Research
260 Laser like focus – The Dogsled Derby
263 Capture the magic moments - Don't Chase Happiness
267 How thoughts can change your life – Brian Tracey
270 An amazing story – Bill Porter Cerebral Palsy
273 You can grow old gracefully – 96 Years Old and Happy
276 If you think you can – Franklin D. Roosevelt
279 It's all about perspective – You Have the Power
282 Pressure can help – The Butterfly and the Cocoon
285 Thinking outside the box – Black and White Pebbles
288 See the bigger picture – Change your focus
291 Achieve more – Justice Oliver Wendell Holmes
294 Fulfil your potential – Barnyard Chicken and the Eagle
298 Don't listen to the dream killers – Apple Computers
301 It's not what happens – Near Fatal Accident
304 Encourage others – The Group of Frogs
307 Leave a legacy – Wolfgang Amadeus Mozart
310 Keep going to the end – Stay in the Game
313 Hard work and integrity – Chuck Swindoll
316 Don't miss your opportunity – Hershey's chocolate
319 Living a happy and content life – The Fisherman
322 Stress paralyses you – The Glass of Water
325 It's not all bad – Forbes Magazine

HOW TO USE THIS BOOK

Reflection, Inspiration, and Action...

There are three ways you can use this book to help you on your journey to Mental Resilience in 100 days. There is no right or wrong way. What's important is that you decide whether to simply read and absorb each daily story or use it as a 'plan of action' with daily reflections or actions. We wanted to give you the choice.

1.   You can read each of the 100 stories that are linked to one of the core principles of Mental Resilience, and these are specifically written for you to read one each day for 100 days. Read each one over the next 100 days, and I'm sure they will resonate with you; you will understand the learning, and then you can apply those learnings at your own time and pace.

2.   You can read one story each day and then use the space provided to write down your reflection. How did you feel reading it? What was YOUR personal takeaway from the story? What or who did it make you think about?

3. This third level of interaction is when you read the story, write down your reflections from it, and then there is a whole section at the back of the book for you to note down your personal TOP 10 positive actions you might want to commit to taking.

Whichever way you decide to use the book, I'm sure you will find inspiration from each daily reading. These readings are designed to be a 'quick daily read' and should be no more than a 2-minute read in the morning and then a few minutes at the end of the day for reflection, a great way to start and end each day.

You will notice that each of the principles of Mental Resilience is repeated several times throughout the book. This is deliberate to ensure that you internalise these crucial principles.

The Amazing Science behind Mental Resilience and A Positive Frame of Mind.

For some people who have embraced the principles of Mental Resilience, they need no evidence of its real and true power. For others, it can seem hard to believe that simply the way you think can have a direct impact on your mental and physical health and your material world around you.

In this book, you will read 100 stories about people who have, sometimes without even knowing it, used the power of Mental Resilience, which resulted in a mental change first and then a real physical change to their lives or their particular situation. The key here is that it all started in the MIND.

We now have the science to back up the impact a "positive" mindset can have on you, your health, and your life. The opposite is true, therefore, and we can also see the evidence of what effect a "negative" mindset can have.

Research conducted by R. McCraty and D. Childre in 2004 (Authors of The Grateful Heart: The Psychophysiology of Appreciation) demonstrating the power of Positive or Negative Thoughts.

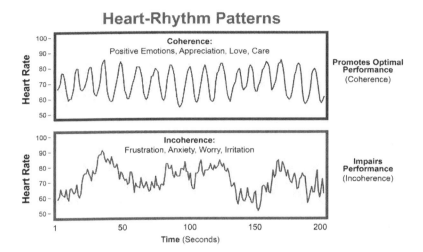

From this data, we can see that negative thoughts and emotions create erratic heart rates, and they can lead to very different "performance" outcomes or feelings.

Steady, calm heart rates can lead to Coherence (Positive Emotions, Appreciation, Love, Care), and the results of this are **Optimal Performance**. The opposite of this is erratic and fluctuating heart rates leading to Incoherence (Frustration, Anxiety, Worry, and Irritation) and therefore **Impaired Performance**.

During stress and negative emotions, when the heart rhythm pattern is erratic and disordered, the corresponding pattern of neural signals traveling from the heart to the brain inhibits higher cognitive functions.

This limits our ability to think clearly, remember, learn, reason, and make effective decisions. The heart's input to the brain during stressful or negative emotions also has a profound effect on the brain's emotional processes – actually serving to reinforce the emotional experience of stress."

Neuropsychologist Rick Hanson, Ph.D., a Senior Fellow of the Greater Good Science Center at UC Berkeley, and New York Times best-selling author, says that:

"When we experience uplifting emotions such as gratitude, joy, compassion, and love; our heart rhythm pattern becomes highly ordered, looking like a smooth, harmonious wave"

It's no wonder that positive emotions feel so good. They actually help our body's systems synchronise and work better.

Study by Harvard Demonstrating the Health Benefits of Optimism

Another very detailed study from Harvard analysed data between 2004 to 2012 from 70,000 women enrolled in the Nurses' Health Study, a long-running study tracking women's health via surveys every two years. The study looked at the participant's levels of optimism and other factors that might play a role in how optimism may affect mortality risks, such as race, high blood pressure, diet, and physical activity.

They found that amongst the 70,000 women, the ones that were more optimistic had a significantly reduced risk of dying from several major causes of death over an eight-year period compared to the women who were less optimistic.

"The most optimistic women (the top quartile) had a nearly 30% lower risk of dying from any of the diseases analysed in the study compared with the least optimistic (the bottom quartile)". The most optimistic women had a 16% lower risk of dying from cancer, 38% lower risk of dying from heart disease, 39% lower risk of dying from a stroke, and 52% lower risk of dying from infection.

Study by the Mayo Clinic Demonstrating the Health Benefits of Positive Thinking.
The Mayo Clinic published some findings in February 2017 with some 4,500 physicians, scientists, and researchers sharing their expertise along with another 58,400 administrative and allied health staff. They cited The Health Benefits of Positive Thinking and listed what they believed were the benefits that Positive Thinking may provide. They were: 1. Increased Life Span. 2. Lower Rates of Depression. 3. Lower Rates of Distress. 4. Greater Resistance to the Common Cold. 5. Better Psychological and Physical Well-being. 6. Better Cardiovascular Health and Reduced Risk of Death

from Cardiovascular Disease and 7. Better Coping Skills During Hardships and Times of Stress.

Study Demonstrating the Power of Positive Visualizations

In this positive thinking study, published in March 2016 in the Journal of Behaviour Research and Therapy, researchers from Kings College in London tested 102 subjects diagnosed with an anxiety disorder. They asked one group to visualize an image of a positive outcome to each of the three worries they'd had in the past week, another group to think of positive verbal outcomes, and the last group to visualize any positive image whenever they started to worry. The two groups that visualized a positive image, whether it related to a specific worry or not, reported greater happiness, restfulness, and decreased anxiety.

Study Demonstrating the Effects of Stress

Researchers, led by Dr Segerstrom at the University of Kentucky, analysed over 300 separate studies in the previous 30 years within the psychological community of the effects of stress on humans and concluded that when people face a stressful situation, they get a burst of adrenaline that boosts their immune system and helps them to better deal with the immediate situation. But, over time, if they continue to stress about an event, their immune systems break down, causing illness, depression, and anxiety disorder. If you cannot change your situation, change your thinking about it.

Study Demonstrating the Power of a Positive Outlook

This review, published in the December 2005 issue of Psychological Bulletin, examined studies of over 275,000 people and found that the happiest people owe their success, in part, to their optimism and positive outlook. Dr. Lyubomirsky, head researcher from UC Riverside concluded: "When people feel happy, they tend to feel confident, optimistic and energetic and others find them likeable and sociable. Happy people are thus able to benefit from these perceptions."

A pretty compelling list, I'm sure you'll agree.

Some may think that controlling your mind, having a more positive outlook, and being more Mentally Resilient is a spiritual thing (and in some cases, it can be). If you take a closer look, you will see that Science can back up the fact that having a more Positive Mindset can change your mind, make you healthier, and could, literally, change your life.

FIRE IN HER HEART

9-year-old Lesia Cartelli and her cousin were playing in their grandparents' basement when a gas leak ignited, causing the whole house to blow up. The explosion threw many of the 9 family members in the home across the street.

Already a fighter, Lesia pulled herself out of the rubble. Flames still covered her little body, so she rolled in the dirt and snow to put them out.

"It was all face, hands, back, and parts where I had synthetic on where the blast had burned around my waist," she says.

Lesia spent several months in the hospital, undergoing surgeries and skin grafts. Once released, Lesia's scars drew stares and questions from people, so she started isolating herself.

"When I was burned, everything in my life changed," she said. "My friendships changed. I hated going to school. You are coping with things you never had to cope with before. People staring at you. People asking questions. Why do you look like that?"

Lesia could have remained withdrawn her whole life. When bad things happen, we can always choose to retreat or give our pain purpose. Lesia chose the latter, realizing she was put on this Earth to do more than just survive.

"My life got better when I started to look at my life as a gift," Lesia said.

Lesia started Angel Faces, a national non-profit organization offering week-long supportive retreats for adolescent female burn victims. These retreats, for girls ranging from ages 11-19, provide seminars to help the girls heal emotionally.

"The common denominator among burn survivors is the feeling of being alone - even when they have amazing support at home," says Dana Kuhn, director of programs at the Burn Institute in San Diego. "Once you go to a gathering of survivors, you no longer have that sense of being alone."

Volunteers and therapists at the Angel Faces Retreats help the girls accept their new appearance, working to boost their self-esteem, as well as providing ways they can live a positive life. Those who attend describe it as a life-changing experience. And they point to Lesia as a huge inspiration.

As a woman burned in a gas explosion, Lesia is able to connect with these young ladies on a personal level, as someone who knows what they're going through.

Thought for Today

It's not what happens to you but how you respond which counts

How do you respond when things go wrong? Do you take stock and see the positive, or do you struggle? Today ponder on the story of Lesia Cartelli and see if you can gain some inspiration to tackle your difficult situations. See if you can find a seed of something positive in your negative situation.

Today's Reflection

_____

_____

_____

_____

_____

_____

_____

_____

_____

_____

THE POWER OF PERSISTENCE

*T*yler Perry had a rough childhood. He was physically and sexually abused growing up, got kicked out of high school, and tried to commit suicide twice—once as a preteen and again at 22. At 23, he moved to Atlanta and took up odd jobs as he started working on his stage career.

In 1992 he wrote, produced, and starred in his first theatre production, 'I Know I've Been Changed,' somewhat informed by his difficult upbringing. Perry put all his savings into the show, and it failed miserably; the run lasted just one weekend, and only 30 people came to watch.

He kept up with the production, working more odd jobs and often sleeping in his car to get by. Six years later, Perry finally broke through when, on its seventh run, the show became a success.

He's since gone on to have an extremely successful career as a director, writer, and actor. In fact, Perry was named Forbes' highest-paid man in entertainment in 2011.

Persistence is a wonderful attribute which helps us to achieve success. If you are persistent you will be more successful in life. I needed it to make it to the level of international and professional basketball. I have also needed it to continue to build my business at the age of 66.

I needed it when I was speaking free of charge to 7 people at a Rotary Club meeting, and 3 of them fell asleep. I needed it when I couldn't get any bookings, and I had to paint and decorate for 4 long years. I needed it when Coronavirus hit, and all my bookings for the year were cancelled.

It's taken me a long time to develop my Mental Resilience Masterclass and Keynote talk, and all this work is finally paying off. It is a joy to see the techniques I teach impacting people's lives. It would have been easy to give up when people were telling me to retire gracefully and enjoy a nice quiet life. But I am 66 and just warming up!

Thought for Today

Persistence is one of the key attributes to success

What is your persistence like? Today think about times when you have tried something and succeeded after persisting for a while. How did it feel? Is there something in your world right now that you could focus on and apply some persistence to see if it can come to fruition?

Today's Reflection

_____

_____

_____

_____

_____

_____

_____

_____

_____

_____

AN ENCOURAGING WORD

I read this account of the famous actress Emily Blunt who was encouraged by a teacher who completely changed her life. She lacked confidence, but a few words of encouragement from this unsung hero changed everything.

Emily Olivia Leah Blunt was born on 23 February 1983, in Wandsworth, London, to Oliver Simon Peter Blunt, a barrister and Joanna, a teacher and one-time actress. Emily has three siblings, an older sister named Felicity, a younger brother named Sebastian, and a younger sister named Susannah.

'Before Blunt was getting nominated for Golden Globes and landing leading roles on the stage and big screen, she could barely carry a conversation with her classmates: Between ages 7 and 14, Emily had a major stutter.

As she told W magazine, "I was a smart kid and had a lot to say, but I just couldn't say it. It would just haunt me. I never thought I'd be able to sit and talk to someone like I'm talking to you right now."

But that all changed when one of her junior high teachers encouraged her to try out for the school play—a totally unappealing feat given the fact that she had such a hard time communicating.

But the teacher kept gently pressing and suggested she try accents and character voices to help get the words out— and it worked. By the end of her teens, Blunt had overcome her stutter and went on to achieve the successful career she has now.'

In August 2000, she got an opportunity to demonstrate her acting skills in the 'Edinburgh Festival' where she caught the attention of an actor and agent named Kenneth McReddie. Kenneth helped Emily make a mark in London's theatre district, the 'West End,' and BBC.

Blunt found herself sharing screen space with the likes of Tom Cruise and Meryl Streep. Also, she walked away with a 'Critics' Choice Movie Award' for 'Best Actress.'

She continued to impress fans and critics alike with her performances in films, such as 'The Huntsman: Winter's War' and 'The Girl on the Train.'

This is a great example of how key people in your life can literally change the course of your future. The teacher offered her the challenge to test herself in the school play to break the speech impediment. She must have been petrified, but she took the challenge on. That teacher changed her life forever.

Thought for Today

Sometimes all we need is encouragement and a kind word.

Today think back through your life and try to remember anyone who has helped you along your journey. What did they say? What did they do? As you go forward in your life, be aware of anyone you can encourage or help in some way. You could be the catalyst that changes a life for the better.

Today's Reflection

_____

_____

_____

_____

_____

_____

_____

_____

_____

_____

_____

THE RIGHT ATTITUDE

It makes me realise why I am so passionate about what I do and why I have this plan to be doing this until at least the age of 80. Now in my sixties, I love having a reason to get up in the morning and achieve things during the day, which make a positive difference to people. Recently I came across this little story, which I feel captures the essence of successful, happy living.

What Am I?

"I am seldom considered, though I do more to influence everything about you than virtually any one thing in your life. I often control the time you get up in the morning, the time you go to sleep, what you eat and drink, and the very thought that runs through your head.

I can make you either happy or sad, loving or hateful, cheerful or remorseful, congenial, or spiteful and, in doing so, control the very capacity that you have for success.

No, you don't often think of me. Instead, you BLAME the problem I create on the shortcoming of others, or the state of the economy, or your family or a million other reasons. Often at times unable to find anyone else to BLAME, you look for shortcomings within yourself on which to lay the BLAME.

When my impact on your life is fully considered in your every thought and action, when you are mindful of my awesome power, when you nurture and groom me for positive use in your life, I can become more contagious than the most prolific disease ever witnessed by man. My influence will spread to every person you come in contact with.

Groomed and nurtured in a positive manner, there will be no person or obstacle that can stand in the way of my success or fail to be impacted for the better. Who am I? I am Your Attitude."

As one of my favourite motivation speakers, Zig Ziglar, once said, 'Your Attitude determines your Altitude,' and it is so true. Maintain a positive attitude and watch what starts to happen in your life. These are the techniques and principles I teach, and I know it works!

Thought for Today

The right attitude will take you further in life and you will be happier.

Today think about your attitude. Do you have a positive attitude or a negative attitude? Research has demonstrated that a positive attitude has an impact on energy levels, health and happiness. From today see if you can nurture a more positive attitude and then observe how this affects your life. It takes time but it's worth it.

Today's Reflection

_____

_____

_____

_____

_____

_____

_____

_____

_____

DEALING WITH REJECTION

Sylvester Stallone has been a household name for decades after the monster success of the Rocky franchise that began in the 1970s. Not only did he star in these movies as Rocky, but he also directed, produced, and wrote most of the films.

Rocky was his first big hit that made him a certified movie star and would go on film in countless action films.

Today, at age 72, he is still acting, writing, and directing feature films. While he makes success look easy, that was not always the case. Here is the unbelievable inspiring story of Sylvester Stallone — a true rags to riches story.

Like many actors, Stallone struggled at the beginning of his Hollywood career. But his struggles were more than most. He was so broke that he became homeless, sold his wife's jewellery, and even sold his dog for $25 as he had no money to feed him anymore.

He said that was the lowest moment of his entire life and walked away crying.

A few weeks after the tragic event, he watched a Muhammad Ali boxing match that inspired him to write Rocky. He was so inspired that he wrote the entire script in less than a day! Studios loved the script but didn't love Sylvester Stallone's one request — to be the main lead in the movie.

He was offered over $300,000 for the script but still said no — despite being dead broke! He knew that this movie was his ticket to success. After enough time, a studio agreed to let him star and only gave him $35,000 for the script. Several things happened.

First, he went back to the place he sold his dog, waited around long enough, and was able to buy him back.... for $15,000! But it wasn't a problem as Rocky went on to make history. With a small budget of one million dollars, it went on to gross $225 million, be nominated for several Oscars, and yield six sequels.

"Every time I've failed, people had me out for the count, but I always come back." Sylvester Stallone.

The best part of this inspirational story is that you can learn two main principles to help you succeed:

1. Always Believe in Yourself
2. Life Can Be Hard Before It's Easy

As motivational speaker Les Brown said,

> *"You have the ability to do more than you could ever begin to imagine."*

Thought for Today

It may be tough but now, but good times are ahead

This has been an extremely tough year with Coronavirus, but we are seeing light at the end of the tunnel. If we focus on the devastation and potential recession, we feel bad. If we focus on the recovery and believe that it will turn around, we feel good. What you focus on is what you feel - today, focus on the good things to feel better and have more energy.

Today's Reflection

_____

_____

_____

_____

_____

_____

_____

_____

_____

_____

_____

AMAZING DETERMINATION

R ecently I came across this story of persistence, which is quite amazing.

A PERSON could know South Korea for a long time without knowing Wanju, an obscure county 112 miles south of Seoul. And, at least until recently, a person could know a lot about Wanju without ever hearing of Cha Sa-soon, a 69-year-old woman who lives alone in the mountain-ringed village of Sinchon.

Now, however, Ms. Cha is an unlikely national celebrity.

This diminutive woman, now known nationwide as "Grandma Cha Sa-soon", has achieved a record that causes people here to first shake their heads with astonishment and then smile: She failed her driver's test hundreds of times but never gave up. Finally, she got her licence on her 960th try.

For three years starting in April 2005, she took the theory test once a day, five days a week. After that, her pace slowed to about twice a week. But she never quit.

Hers is a fame based not only on sheer doggedness, a quality held in high esteem by Koreans, but also on the universal human sympathy for a monumental and in her case, cheerful loser.

"When she finally got her license, we all went out and hugged her, giving her flowers," said Park Su-Yeon, an instructor at Jeonbuk Driving School, which Ms. Cha once attended. "It felt like a huge burden falling off our back. We didn't have the guts to tell her to quit because she kept showing up."

Once she finally got her licence, in May, Hyundai-Kia Automotive Group, South Korea's leading carmaker started an online campaign asking people to post messages of congratulations. Thousands poured in. In early August, Hyundai presented Ms. Cha with a $16,800 car.

Ms. Cha said she had always envied people who could drive, but it was not until she was in her 60s that she got around to trying for a license.

I wonder how many times I would have attempted this exam if I were in her shoes – 10, 20, 50? Determination is one of the keys to success, but it is extremely difficult to remain determined as you face adversity after adversity. It is much easier to give up, but the people who succeed in life don't. They keep getting back up again and again until they finally breakthrough.

The feeling of achievement you experience when you eventually succeed is simply amazing.

Thought for Today

Determination will take you places you never dreamed of.

Do you have the determination to keep going when you can't see the finish line? Today think about Grandma Cha and try to imagine what kept her going for 3 years, never giving up. Did she visualise driving a car which she had desired for so long? Was this mental image in her mind so strong that it kept her going failure after failure?

Today's Reflection

_____

_____

_____

_____

_____

_____

_____

_____

_____

_____

MENTAL MOVIES

I came across this great example of visualisation from the comedian and film actor Jim Carrey.

When Carrey was 14 years old, his father lost his job, and his family hit rough times. They moved into a VW van on a relative's lawn.

The young aspiring comedian—who was so dedicated to his craft that he mailed his resume to The Carroll Burnett Show just a few years earlier, at age 10—took an eight-hours-per-day factory job after school to help make ends meet.

At age 15, Carrey performed his comedy routine onstage for the first time—in a suit, his mom made him—and totally bombed, but he was undeterred. The next year, at 16, he quit school to focus on comedy full time.

He moved to L.A. shortly after, where he would park on Mulholland Drive every night and visualize his success. One of these nights, he wrote himself a check for $10,000,000 for "Acting Services Rendered," which he dated for Thanksgiving 1995.

Just before that date, he hit his payday with Dumb and Dumber. He put the deteriorated cheque, which he'd kept in his wallet the whole time, in his father's casket when he died.

The Power of the Mental Movie

Jim Carrey had an amazing mental movie playing in his head. He saw himself receiving that amount in the future. He believed that he would receive this and he told people that one day he would be paid this amount.

I know that this isn't possible for everyone, but I wonder how far he would have gone in life if he didn't have the vision that one day he would be very successful. This belief took him through the pain of humiliation he experienced as he was regularly booed off the stage.

Without the vision and belief, he would have given up before he broke through to success.

Thought for Today

What Mental Movies do you have running in your mind?

Research shows that positive people are happier, healthier, and achieve more in life. Today I want you to think about the mental movies playing in your mind. What do you focus most on during the day? Do you see the worst outcome each time or the best outcome? From today try to play more positive mental movies and watch what happens.

Today's Reflection

_____

_____

_____

_____

_____

_____

_____

_____

_____

_____

BROKE BUT HE HAD A DREAM

I came across this article about a man with amazing vision and determination, and this article simply tells his amazing story of persistence.

"Once, there was an older man who was broke, living in a tiny house and owned a beat-up car. He was living off of $99 social security checks. At 62 years of age, he decided things had to change. So, he thought about what he had to offer. His friends raved about his chicken recipe. He decided that this was his best shot at making a change.

He left Kentucky and travelled to different states to try to sell his recipe. He told restaurant owners that he had a mouth-watering chicken recipe. He slept in his car every night, and every time he got back in his car with another rejection, he made a note in his notebook.

He offered the recipe to them for free, just asking for a small percentage on the items sold. Sounds like a good deal, right?

Unfortunately, not to most of the restaurants. No one had heard of this older man, and they certainly weren't willing to try his recipe. He was rejected over 1000 times. Even after all of those rejections, he didn't give up. He believed his chicken recipe was something special. He heard the word NO 1009 times before he heard his first yes.

With that one success, Colonel Hartland Sanders changed the way Americans eat chicken. Kentucky Fried Chicken, popularly known as KFC, was born.

Remember, never give up and always believe in yourself in spite of rejection."

These final words are really powerful, 'Never give up and always believe in yourself.' This reminds me of a plaque I have with the following words on it, which I read twice a day, every day.

The words say:

'Go for your Dream and Never give up. Believe in Yourself and the Best is Yet to Come'

If your words are positive, you will achieve more in life than if your words are negative. Only a few years ago, I was decorating with no clients, and my inner dialogue was completely negative. Then I discovered the power of inner dialogue, and I changed my self-talk from negative to positive. Then suddenly everything in my life started to change for the better.

THE KEYS IN THE BOOK

A young man was getting ready to graduate college. For many months he had admired a beautiful sports car in a dealer's showroom. Knowing his father could well afford it, he told him that was all he wanted.

As Graduation Day approached, the young man waited for signs that his father had purchased the car. Finally, on the morning of his graduation, his father called him into his study. His father told him how proud he was to have such a fine son and how much he loved him. He handed his son a beautifully wrapped gift box.

Curious, but disappointed, the young man opened the box and found a beautiful, leather-bound Bible. Angrily, he shouted at his father, "With all your money, you just give me a Bible?" And he stormed out of the house, leaving the holy book and his father behind.

Many years passed. The young man became very successful in business. He had a beautiful home and a wonderful family. But he thought about his father, who had grown old.

He had not seen him since that graduation day. But before he could make arrangements to go to him, he received a telegram telling him his father had died and willed all of his possessions to his son. He needed to come home immediately to take care of things.

When the man arrived at his father's house, sadness and regret filled his heart. Searching through his father's important papers, he found the still new Bible, just as he had left it years before. In tears, he began to turn the pages and read its words.

Something dropped from an envelope taped to the Bible. A car key with a dealer's tag, the same dealer who had the sports car he had desired. On the tag was the date of his graduation, and the words PAID IN FULL.

As I read these words, my heart saddened as this son can never make amends for his reaction to the gift he imagined his father had given him. He wanted the sports car, and his father had bought the car for him, but for a surprise, he had hidden the keys in the Bible.

Pride and hurt stopped them reconnecting, and it damaged them both. How sad that something so small could result in something so huge and life-changing.

Thought for Today

Do you have anyone in your life who you have fallen out with?

Is there a possibility that you can reconnect with them, even if they hurt you?
Who are you going to get in touch with today? There is great joy in healing a broken relationship, and sometimes all it takes is for someone to make the first move. It could be a text, an email, a card in the post, a gift, a phone call, or a surprise visit.

Today's Reflection

_____

_____

_____

_____

_____

_____

_____

_____

_____

_____

Abraham Lincoln:

*"It's not the years in your life that count.
It's the life in your years."*

THE ICE CREAM SUNDAE?

In the days when an ice cream sundae cost much less than now, a 10-year-old boy entered a coffee shop and sat at a table. A waitress put a glass of water in front of him.

"How much is an ice cream sundae?" he asked. "Fifty cents," replied the waitress.
The little boy pulled his hand out of his pocket and studied the coins in it. "How much is a plain dish of ice cream?" he inquired.

Other people were waiting to be served, and the waitress was growing impatient. "Thirty-five cents," she brusquely replied. The little boy again counted his coins. "I'll have the plain ice cream," he said.

The waitress brought the ice cream, put the bill on the table, and walked away. The boy finished the ice cream, paid the cashier and left.

When the waitress came back, she began to cry as she wiped down the table.

There, placed neatly beside the empty dish, were two nickels and five pennies. The boy couldn't have the sundae, because he wanted to have enough money left to leave her a tip.

This story brought a tear to my eye for some reason, and I felt emotional. Maybe it was the caring nature of the boy who wanted to bless the waitress with a tip because he knew it was the right thing to do. He was prepared to sacrifice the extra enjoyment of a sundae so he could leave a tip.

Maybe it was a reminder of when I have been blessed with some kindness in the past. The boy likely learned this from his parents or significant others. We model people's behaviour if we are exposed to those behaviours for long enough. Without doubt, he had been exposed to this tradition of leaving a tip for service.

It is a timely reminder that there is always room for kindness and doing the right thing. When studies are carried out on happy people, they tend to be kind and generous. When we do something for someone to bless them, we not only feel good about it, but something good often happens to us down the line.

Thought for Today

Find an opportunity to do one small act of kindness today.

Today try to find someone to bless with an act of kindness, then see how you feel afterwards. I believe that the way to true happiness is helping others. It could be someone at home or someone at work. It could be a complete stranger who you meet, and it could be as simple as opening a door for them or a word of encouragement.

Today's Reflection

_____

_____

_____

_____

_____

_____

_____

_____

_____

_____

_____

CAR CRASH IN ASDA

I crashed my lovely car at 3 am one Saturday in June 2011, in my local Asda car park! I'd been packing for a straight 27 hours in a rush to get everything ready for the move to Nottingham. I'd decided to go and live with my mum. I wanted to keep her company and look after her to the best of my abilities. My father died last year, and she was very lonely, and I knew she would appreciate the company.

It was now 3 am, and I was so tired that I thought I'd pop to the 24hr McDonald's for a coffee and a short break. On the way, I diverted to Asda to get some drinks and crashed into a lamp post in the middle of the empty car park. The only explanation I can give is that I fell asleep at the wheel and went straight into it! The impact was so severe that I wrote the car off.

I sat there in shock as I hadn't finished packing yet, and I had to pick up the hire van at 7.45 am - less than 4 hours away. After discussing the situation with the security men, we pushed the car to the side of the car park, and I walked home in the rain to phone the insurance company. I remember the rain getting in my shoe through a hole in the sole.

At 7.30 am, the taxi I'd ordered arrived to take me to pick up the van. The driver said that he recognised me, that he had seen me in McDonald's where I often work on my laptop. I was still in shock, and my mind was spinning as to how I was going to sort everything out with the car later on. I asked him how he was, and he said that his friend, who was always with him, wasn't doing too well as his daughter had been recently murdered - and they couldn't bury her as the investigation was still on-going.

The impact of this was immediate and put into perspective the magnitude of my problem compared to his. I will get another car, but his friend won't get his daughter back. Following this, my whole attitude to the car problem changed completely.

Thought for Today

It's all about perspective

Think about a situation right now that is bothering you and see if you can put it in perspective compared to other things. Look at the big picture and see if you will even remember this in 6 months. Is this situation life or death, or will it be resolved eventually? Sometimes just comparing to more serious situations helps you deal with it.

Today's Reflection

_____

_____

_____

_____

_____

_____

_____

_____

_____

_____

_____

THE POWER OF GRATITUDE

After I had finished a coaching session in London one day, I was travelling back to St Pancras train station when I saw two blind people being helped onto the train. They sat opposite me, and what I witnessed had quite an impact on me.

They both had white sticks which they folded away and then proceeded to have a wonderful conversation, which was full of humour. They were clearly well acquainted, and I don't know if they were a couple or just friends, but they were very comfortable in each other's company. What impacted me was they were happy with life, laughing and joking about things, sometimes talking quietly, sometimes loudly, but they were engrossed in each other's conversations.

This reminded me of how we can re-frame negative things into positives, even in the most difficult of circumstances. It's incredible how we can adapt to situations that can be devastating. I don't know if this man and woman were born blind or whether it happened as they went through their lives. Either way, it must be a massive challenge to accept such a situation and live life on your own terms, especially in a world that is so reliant on all your senses, particularly sight.

We have a choice each day to consider what we can do rather than what we can't do. If you focus on the negative things in your life, there is a danger of becoming a victim. You can choose to look at what you can do and be grateful for all the opportunities you have.

So what are you grateful for in your life? What are you taking for granted? It's so easy to moan and groan about how difficult things are when, in reality, we are blessed with so many wonderful things.

Thought for Today

Do you find time to be grateful for all the good things in your life?

Take some time this week to look at your world and identify what is good in it and be grateful. We are often so busy that we don't have time to stop and appreciate the wonderful things we have in life. Think about the people around you and the home you own or rent. Maybe the beautiful things in nature or the TV and food you enjoy.

Today's Reflection

_____

_____

_____

_____

_____

_____

_____

_____

_____

_____

_____

HELEN KELLER – A REMARKABLE STORY!

"*Helen Keller was born 27 June 1880 in Tuscumbia, Alabama. When she was only 19 months old, she experienced a severe childhood illness, which left her deaf and blind (only a very partial sight).*

For the first few years of her life, she was only able to communicate with her family through a rudimentary number of signs; she had a little more success communicating with the six-year-old daughter of the family cook.

However, unable to communicate properly, she was considered to be badly behaved; for example, eating from the plates of anyone on the table with her fingers.

*In 1886, Helen was sent to see an eye, ear, and nose specialist in Baltimore. He put them in touch with **Alexander Graham Bell**, who was currently investigating issues of deafness and sound (he would also develop the first telephone).*

Alexander Bell helped Keller to visit the Perkins Institute for the Blind, and this led to a long relationship with Anne Sullivan – who was a former student herself.

Sullivan was visually impaired and, aged only 20, and with no prior experience, she set about teaching Helen how to communicate. The two maintained a long relationship of 49 years.

In the beginning, Keller was frustrated by her inability to pick up the hand signals that Sullivan was giving. However, after a frustrating month, Keller picked up on Sullivan's system of hand signals by distinguishing the word water.

Sullivan poured water over Keller's left hand and wrote out on her right hand the word 'water.' This helped Helen to fully comprehend the system, and she was soon able to identify a variety of household objects.

Keller made rapid progress and quickly overcame her bad habits. She became proficient in Braille and was able to begin a fruitful education, despite her disability. Keller made more progress than anyone expected. She would later learn to write with a Braille typewriter.

Keller became a proficient writer and speaker. In 1903, she published an autobiography 'The Story of My Life' It recounted her struggles to overcome her disabilities and the way it forced her to look at life from a different perspective.

"When one door of happiness closes, another opens; but often we look so long at the closed door that we do not see the one which has been opened for us." – Helen Keller.

Thought for Today

It's not what happens to you in life but how you respond, which makes the difference.

Mindset is everything, and once we understand this, our lives can be transformed. No matter what our current circumstances are, we can change them for the better with the right Mindset and Mental Resilience. To put what Helen faced in perspective, close your eyes, and put your fingers in your ears. This is what her life was like – now try to imagine the difficulties she faced.

Today's Reflection

_____

_____

_____

_____

_____

_____

_____

_____

_____

_____

THE LUMBERJACK STORY

It was the annual lumberjack competition, and the final was between an older experienced lumberjack and a younger, stronger, lumberjack. The rule of the competition was quite simple - whoever could fell the most trees in a day was the winner.

The younger lumberjack was full of enthusiasm and went off into the wood and set to work straight away. He worked all through the day and all through the night. As he worked, he could hear the older lumberjack working in another part of the forest.

At regular intervals, throughout the day, the noise of trees being felled coming from the other part of the forest would stop. The younger lumberjack took heart from this as it meant the older lumberjack was taking a rest, whereas he could use his superior youth and strength and stamina to keep going.

At the end of the competition, the younger lumberjack felt confident he had won; he looked in front of him at the piles of felled trees that were the result of his superhuman effort.

At the medal ceremony, he stood on the podium, confident and expecting to be awarded the prize. Next to him stood the older lumberjack who looked surprisingly less exhausted than he felt.

When the results were read out, he was devastated to hear that the older lumberjack had chopped down significantly more trees than he had. He turned to the older lumberjack and said;

"How can this be? I heard you take a rest every hour and I worked continuously through the night, once more I am stronger and fitter than you, old man".

The older lumberjack turned to him and said, "Every hour I took a break to rest, I would sharpen my axe."

Taking time out to change things may slow you down initially, but once you have made changes that can improve your life, you will move forward more productively.

Thought for Today

Do you take time to rest and recover?

Do you take time to rest and plan your day (sharpen your axe)? Today think about your work/life balance and make sure you are resting and recovering properly. You will achieve more in less time by planning your day and taking time to rest. When you are tired, it takes you much longer to complete a task. For peak performance, it is far better to take breaks.

Today's Reflection

_____

_____

_____

_____

_____

_____

_____

_____

_____

_____

_____

_____

THE FUTILITY OF FAME AND FORTUNE

Society's fascination with Hollywood and celebrities has gone a little crazy. Millions idolise those who have achieved fame and fortune, yet stardom does not provide the satisfaction it advertises. Marilyn Monroe could have told us that. So could Elvis Presley and Michael Jackson.

Consider the adoration accorded to Muhammad Ali in his prime. He was known as the 'prize-fighter who couldn't be beaten.' His picture appeared on the cover of Sports Illustrated more times than any other athlete in history. Wherever he went, the cameras followed. But wealth and fame cannot buy good health, and he fell victim to the ravages of Parkinson's disease.

Sportswriter Gary Smith spent some time with the ailing fighter at his home and asked to see his trophy room. Ali escorted him to a dark, damp barn beside the house. There leaning against a wall was a board displaying mementoes – photos of the 'Thrilla in Manilla,' pictures of Ali dancing and punching, and hoisting championship belts he had won over his head.

The pictures were smeared with the white streaks caused by pigeons that had made their home in the rafters. Ali picked up the board and turned it around, face to the wall. Then as he started to leave, Smith heard him mumble, "I had the whole world, and it wasn't nuthin, look at me now."

This account fills me with sadness and reminds me of how fragile life can be. The once-great Ali, who was an example of peak mental and physical condition, had been reduced to a person who had a broken body. Parkinsons is a cruel illness that slowly destroys the body.

Our minds are so easily distracted, habitually examining past events and trying to anticipate the future, and constantly multitasking. It's easy to lose awareness of the present moment as we become lost in our efforts to juggle work, home, finances, and other conflicting demands.

Thought for Today

What are your thoughts on fame and fortune?

Do you see beyond money and owning shiny things?
Is there more to a happy life? Take some time out
to practise staying in the moment. There are many
mindfulness ideas these days – find one that suits
you. Pause for a moment to observe the beauty
in nature or a close relationship. Focus on your
breathing or just listen to the sounds around you.

Today's Reflection

_____

_____

_____

_____

_____

_____

_____

_____

_____

_____

_____

_____

_____

STAND AND DELIVER

"Encouragement can work miracles. In the movie Stand and Deliver, high school teacher Jaime Escalante has two students in his class named Johnny. One is a happy child and an excellent student; the other spends his time messing around and getting into trouble.

When the Parent Teacher Association held its first meeting of the year, a mother came up to Jaime and asked, 'How's my son, Johnny getting along?' Jaime mistakenly assumed she was the mother of the better student, so he replied, 'I can't tell you how much I enjoy him. I'm so glad he is in my class'.

The next day 'problem Johnny' came to Jaime and said, 'My mom told me what you said about me last night, I haven't ever had a teacher who wanted me in his class.' The result? He completed his assignments that day and brought in his completed homework the next morning.

A few weeks later, he had become one of Jaime's hardest working students – and one of his best friends. His life had been turned around because of an accidental word of encouragement."

It works like this: When you look for the good in a person and express it, you give them something to live up to. In other words, you motivate them to be better than they are.

This is an excellent example of the power of encouragement, which is something I love to demonstrate with people I meet. I make it a point to comment on something positive I see about them, and I want them to leave feeling better about themselves. The impact words can have is massive, and they can have a positive or a negative effect.

Thought for Today

Can you think of anyone that you can encourage today?

By choosing to find strengths in people and making them aware of these, you will have a powerful impact which can affect their lives forever. Today think of someone who you could encourage. It could be a young person like a son, daughter, nephew, or niece. It could be someone you know or someone you meet on the street.

Today's Reflection

_____

_____

_____

_____

_____

_____

_____

_____

_____

_____

_____

A TRIP TO POLAND CHANGED EVERYTHING

A fortuitous trip to Poland to meet my uncle, who was 6ft 9inches tall and played for the Polish Army basketball team, changed my life. A few words of encouragement from him lit a fire within and gave me a glimmer of hope, which I grasped with both hands. The words he spoke were louder than the words spoken by those captains in PE, and it totally transformed me and my future.

This one moment of encouragement eventually led me to play basketball for England and play professionally for Sunderland. I had a fantastic career, and this has now led me to run my speaking and coaching business and travelling across the world to spread the word on the importance of looking after your mental resilience. I wish my uncle were still alive because I never fully appreciated the effect of his words until the last few years.

When I was 12 years of age, I attended a PE lesson at school where we were lined up against the wall, and four boys were picked out to be captains. They then selected a boy from a wall one by one until there was only one boy left. This boy was the one who wasn't wanted by anyone, and that boy was me.

This had a huge impact on me, and my confidence drained away from me - from that moment on, I never attended another Games lesson. I pretended to be injured, ill, I forgot my kit, or I simply chose detention for refusing to be put through that humiliation again.

Then a few months later, in Poland, I experienced the exact opposite with my uncle, who fed me positive words, and that changed everything.

My negative anchor was set in PE when I wasn't chosen by any of the captains to be in their teams. I hate to think where my life would be now if I hadn't met my uncle.

Self-talk or your Inner Voice is immensely powerful, whether it is positive or negative. I have created a new inner voice, and because of this positive inner voice, I can now speak to hundreds of people in an audience and enjoy it. It allows me to perform well in any pressure situations and has completely destroyed my negative anchor.

Thought for Today

Can you think of a negative experience that made you feel inadequate or a failure? Has this created a negative anchor which is affecting your life?

Your past experiences create your belief system. What people have said to you over the years becomes your belief about who you are and what you can achieve. Today observe what you are saying to yourself and try to speak positively about challenges you are facing. Create a few positive statements you can repeat over and over to override the negative anchor.

Today's Reflection

_____

_____

_____

_____

_____

_____

_____

_____

_____

THE IMPORTANCE OF SETTING GOALS

I remember reading a newspaper when England was getting ready to play Iceland, and Wales was preparing for Northern Ireland. The games were ones where both teams should have won, and England clearly had the easier match. Checking FIFA world rankings, England was ranked 11, and Iceland was ranked 34. Whereas Wales was ranked 26, and Northern Ireland was ranked 25.

England should have won comfortably, and Wales should have struggled to win. But neither of those things happened, and I believe it was the mindset that determined the eventual outcome. England lost 2-1 to Iceland and was knocked out of the European Championship, and Wales beat Ireland 1-0 to progress to the last 8 where they faced Russia.

I noticed in this newspaper article two things which stood out to me. One was an interview with Wayne Rooney, and the other was with Gareth Bale.

Rooney's interview focussed on his determination to do well in the competition and all credit to him for that. *"FA chairman Greg Dyke said boss Roy Hodgson could earn a new contract with a decent quarter-final display – **even if England lose**. But Rooney was in no mood to settle for gallant failure – **even though Hodgson himself would not set a target for success in France."***

This comment said everything you need to know about why England yet again failed to fulfil their potential. As the great motivation speaker Zig Ziglar once said, *"how can you hit a target you don't have?"* If Hodgson wasn't confident enough to step out and aim for a quarter or semi-final target, then what does that say to the players?

Bale revealed that Wales had been inspired by the class of 58 in a bid for Euro glory. The Dragons squad got ready for their crucial clash with Russia by watching a new documentary about the nation's most famous team. It was 58 years ago this week that the Wales team reached the quarter-finals of the World Cup. After watching the film, Wales went out and breezed past Russia 3-0.

What a difference in attitude and mindset - one team looked at past glories and believed they could do the same; the other team refused to set a target. Wales then went on to beat Northern Ireland to reach the quarter-finals where they beat Belgium, who was ranked number 2 in the world!

Thought for Today

Do you set goals for yourself? Do you see the value of setting targets?

There is extensive evidence to demonstrate that people who set targets and work towards them achieve a great deal more than those who don't. Today think about something you want to achieve and set a target to achieve this. It could be setting a date to start or to complete a project. It could be scheduling a meeting to discuss the way forward.

Today's Reflection

_____

_____

_____

_____

_____

_____

_____

_____

_____

_____

_____

_____

THE BIRTH OF A SUPERSTAR!

The above was the headline from a national newspaper about someone I had never heard of before, that caught my eye. The name of this superstar was Adam Peaty, and he had just won the gold medal for the 100m breaststroke final in the Rio Olympics. He also broke his own world record in the process!

I read the article with great interest as I was intrigued by the fact that I wasn't aware of this swimmer, yet here he was an Olympic Gold medal winner and world record holder. I knew without doubt that there was a story of sacrifice, hard work, and mental resilience, and this proved to be the case as I read the article.

It was interesting to read his words in the article as he told of the sacrifices he had made to make this dream come true. The following is taken from the newspaper:

"Aged 15, I hated racing finals because I was so nervous. As I matured, I developed and fought every time," he said. A year later, he dipped below the 60-second barrier for the first time. "I knew that I was fast, so I thought to myself, 'Let's see what the world can do and what I can do, "said Peaty.

I love the phrase he used, "Let's see what the world can do and what I can do." He was saying, let's take on the world and see where we end up. At that moment, he decided to try to become the best in the world, and nothing else would be good enough. By setting this very high goal, he couldn't afford to rest while other swimmers across the world were practising.

This attitude served him well, and he spent the next five years working so hard, sacrificing many things, including his fun time to achieve this dream. His coach Mel Marshall was vital in this success, as she spent thousands of hours with him, encouraging and pushing him. Marshall paid tribute to Peaty's warrior-like attitude in those five years, having sacrificed a social life of any sort since watching London 2012.

Thought for Today

All major achievements involve work and sacrifice.

Today think about how you view working hard and making sacrifices to achieve things in your life. We all must either face the pain of working hard and sacrifice or face the pain of loss. Personally, I don't want to reach the end of my life looking back with regret on the things I could have achieved and where I could have made a difference.

Today's Reflection

_____

_____

_____

_____

_____

_____

_____

_____

_____

_____

_____

_____

Helen Keller:

"Keep your face to the sunshine,
and you cannot see the shadows."

THE PURSUIT OF HAPPINESS.

The movie of this name but spelled Happyness starring Will Smith shows his character Chris refusing to give in as he tried desperately to build a better life for himself and his young son. He was homeless in the early 1980s and had to sleep rough with his small child. In the subway station toilet, the pair would play a game called 'shush,' where they would remain 'invisible' despite what anyone said 'on the other side of the door.' At the time, Chris's son was still in nappies.

Born February 9, 1954, in Milwaukee, Wisconsin, poverty, domestic violence, alcoholism, sexual abuse, and family illiteracy marked Christopher Paul Gardner's childhood. Gardner published his autobiography out of a desire to shed light on these universal issues and show they do not have to define you.

Gardner never knew his father, and lived with his beloved mother, Bettye Jean, when not in foster homes. Gardner is indebted to Bettye Jean for his success as she provided him with strong "spiritual genetics" and taught him that despite where he came from, he could chart another path and attain whatever goals he set for himself.

Fascinated by finance, but without connections, an MBA, or even a college degree, Gardner applied for training programs at brokerages. He eventually won a position as a stockbroker intern at Dean Witter in 1981. While attending the unpaid internship program, Gardner spent a year on the streets with his two-year-old son.

They took refuge at night in a church shelter or the bathroom of a BART subway station in Oakland, California. Nobody at work knew he was homeless and that he had only two suits, which he wore every day for 12 months.

Today, Gardner is a multimillionaire, a motivational speaker, a philanthropist, and an international businessman who is about to launch a private equity fund that will invest solely in South Africa. His partner in the fund? Nelson Mandela. Not bad for a guy who, six years before founding his own brokerage firm, was "fighting, scratching, and crawling my way out of the gutter with a baby on my back."

Chris said, in order to change your life, you need a plan. He called it the C5 complex. "Your plan has to be Clear, Concise, Compelling, Consistent, and Committed," he said.

What a story and what determination. Has anything from this story resonated with you?

Thought for Today

You don't have to be defined by your upbringing.

Do you have a plan which is clear, concise, compelling, consistent, and committed? Today think about what Chris went through to achieve his goals and be inspired into taking some action yourself. Is it worth the pain to get what you want in life? Don't be defined by the label others put on you – design your own label.

Today's Reflection

_____

_____

_____

_____

_____

_____

_____

_____

_____

_____

_____

_____

A NATIONAL HERO

You've probably never heard of him. However, in
Hungary, he's a national hero – everybody there knows
his name and his incredible story. After reading his story,
you'll be inspired by him…

*"In 1938, Karoly Takacs of the Hungarian Army was the top
pistol shooter in the world. He was expected to win the gold
medal in the 1940 Olympic Games scheduled for Tokyo.*

*Those expectations vanished one terrible day just months
before the Olympics. While training with his army squad, a
hand grenade exploded in Takacs' right hand, and Takacs'
shooting hand was blown off.*

*Takacs spent a month in the hospital depressed at both
the loss of his hand and the end to his Olympic dream. At
that point, most people would have quit. And they would
have probably spent the rest of their life feeling sorry for
themselves. Most people would have quit, but not Takacs -
Takacs was a winner.*

*Winners know that they can't let circumstances keep them
down. They understand that life is hard and that they
can't allow life's challenges to beat them. Winners know
in their heart that quitting is not an option. Takacs did
the unthinkable; he picked himself up, dusted himself off,*

and decided to learn how to shoot with his left hand! His reasoning was simple. He just asked himself, "Why not?"

Instead of focusing on what he didn't have – a world-class right shooting hand, he decided to focus on what he did have – incredible mental resilience and a healthy left hand that, with time, could be developed to shoot like a champion. For months Takacs practiced by himself. Maybe he didn't want to subject himself to people who most certainly would have discouraged him from his rekindled dream.

In the spring of 1939, he showed up at the Hungarian National Pistol Shooting Championship. Other shooters approached Takacs to give him their condolences and to congratulate him on having the strength to come and watch them shoot. They were surprised when he said, "I didn't come to watch; I came to compete." They were even more surprised when Takacs won!

In 1948 he qualified for the London Olympics. At the age of 38, Takacs won the Gold Medal and set a new world record in pistol shooting. Four years later, he won the Gold Medal again at the 1952 Helsinki Olympics.

Takacs – a man with the mental resilience to recover QUICKLY.

Thought for Today

Winners bounce back QUICKLY.

Today think about how you respond when you take a hit. Do you bounce back quickly, or do you spiral downward into negativity? What can you do to improve this? When we focus on negative situations, we lose energy, and we can become discouraged. When we focus on positive things, our energy increases. To bounce back, focus on the things going well in your life and use that energy to start again.

Today's Reflection

_____

_____

_____

_____

_____

_____

_____

_____

_____

_____

_____

THE ELEPHANT ROPE

"*As a man was passing the elephants, he suddenly stopped, confused by the fact that these huge creatures were being held by only a small rope tied to their front leg. No chains, no cages. It was obvious that the elephants could, at any time, break away from their bonds, but for some reason, they did not.*

He saw a trainer nearby and asked why these animals just stood there and made no attempt to getaway. "Well," the trainer said, "when they are very young and much smaller we use the same size rope to tie them and, at that age, it's enough to hold them. As they grow up, they are conditioned to believe they cannot break away. They believe the rope can still hold them, so they never try to break free."

The man was amazed. These animals could at any time break free from their bonds, but because they believed they couldn't, they were stuck right where they were. Like the elephants, how many of us go through life hanging onto a belief that we cannot do something simply because we failed at it once before?

Failure is part of learning; we should never give up the struggle in life."

I read the story above recently and was struck by how easily we can create a belief which is real to us but may not, in effect, be real. We may believe that we can't do something because it has always been this way, or we failed before; therefore - it can't be done.

Or we have been told over and over again that we are useless and will never achieve anything in life. But I regularly encourage my coaching clients to challenge those beliefs, and once they do, amazing things start to happen.

It is quite unbelievable how quickly these beliefs become our reality, holding us back from achieving great things in our lives. I have personally had to break many beliefs that held me back over the years. Those of you who know my story know that I couldn't speak in public and had low self-esteem.

Thought for Today

Your belief system is like a rudder to your life.

You can only go as far as you believe you can. Today think about what you believe you can achieve and what you can't. See if there is a limiting belief you have created, which isn't actually real. Challenge this belief by creating a positive inner voice to change this belief. As you repeat the positive words, your belief system will start to change.

Today's Reflection

_____

_____

_____

_____

_____

_____

_____

_____

_____

_____

_____

_____

PLAYING BASKETBALL FOR ENGLAND

When I was a young boy, I decided that no matter what, and whatever obstacles came my way, I would play for England one day.

At first, this seemed to be an impossible dream as I failed to make the grade at the different levels of basketball time and time again. But because of the commitment I'd made to myself, I didn't give up at any stage.

There were many times when I felt like I wasn't progressing as I hoped I would, and I felt like throwing in the towel. But because of the power of commitment, I kept getting back up and trying again. I finally made it to the trials for the England Under 19 team at the age of 17, but I didn't make the cut, and I was devastated.

After a short period of self-pity, I got back up and got going again, this time even more determined to make the team. I received word that I had been selected for trials again and went – this time more resolved than ever to succeed.

Following a weekend of tough trials, we were all called in to hear who had made the cut, and this time I heard my name called out. I was ecstatic! I had a great time playing for the Under 19 England team, then I played for the full England team and represented them in the Commonwealth games.

I was then honoured to sign a professional contract with Sunderland Basketball.

The professional career was very exciting. I played all over the world, culminating in winning the Play-Offs in 1981, where we beat the hot favourites Crystal Palace, who were the best team in the league.

When I turned 60, I committed to a 20-year plan to be speaking on stage at the age of 80. A commitment I made not only to myself but have voiced to many people. I can't guarantee that something won't happen out of my control regarding this, but as far as I am concerned, I'm going for it!

Thought for Today

What can you commit to today, which you have been putting off for a while?

Today think about something you have been putting off for a while and commit to working on this. Share this with someone and see if you can create some momentum. Accountability is powerful and makes a huge difference in starting and completing difficult tasks. When you have someone checking up on you, it gives you extra motivation.

Today's Reflection

_____

_____

_____

_____

_____

_____

_____

_____

_____

THE BOY IN THE FIRE

Negative beliefs can hold you back. I have had to challenge many negative beliefs over the years, but I am living proof that once broken, a new life appears, which is full of sunshine, happiness, and above all, hope.

The following is a truly inspirational story of a young man who didn't believe what the doctors and experts were telling him, and his belief system changed his life forever.

"Once, a young schoolboy was caught in a fire accident in his school and was assumed that he would not live. His mother was told that he was sure to die, for the terrible fire had devastated the lower half of his body. Even if he were to survive, he would be a cripple throughout his life.

But the brave boy didn't want to die, nor did he want to be a cripple. Much to the amazement of his doctor, he did survive. But unfortunately, from his waist down, he had no motor ability. His thin legs just dangled there, lifeless, but his determination to walk was indomitable.

At home, when he was not in bed, he was confined to a wheelchair. One day, he threw himself from the chair and pulled himself across the grass, dragging his legs behind him. He reached the picket fence, raised himself up and then stake by stake, he began dragging himself along the fence, his resolve to walk undeterred.

He did this every day, with faith in himself that he would be able to walk unaided. With his iron persistence and his resolute determination, he did develop the ability to stand up, then to walk haltingly, then to walk by himself and then to run.

He began to walk to school, then run to school, to run for the sheer joy of running. Later in college, he made the track team. In February 1934, in New York City's famed Madison Square Garden, this young man who was not expected to survive, who would surely never walk, who could never hope to run – this determined young man, Dr. Glenn Cunningham, ran the world's fastest mile.

An epitome of the power of positive thinking and faith in one's self, Glenn Cunningham continues to be an inspiration for many."

Thought for Today

If you believe you can achieve something, or you believe you can't, you are right.

Today think about your potential in life and how it is defined by your belief system. You have an inner voice which determines which path you take in life. If you change your inner dialogue, you start to change your path and your ultimate destiny.

Today's Reflection

_____

_____

_____

_____

_____

_____

_____

_____

_____

_____

_____

_____

HE LOST HIS LEGS

"In 1982, something happened to Hugh Herr that changed his life – and ultimately would change the lives of anyone whose physical abilities had been transformed by accident or birth. A prodigious mountain climber, who'd managed to scale a 3.5 km mountain in the Canadian Rockies by the age of 8, Herr became disoriented in a blizzard and was forced to spend three nights in temperatures below minus 29 degrees Centigrade. He lost both legs below the knee.

Many would have become disheartened, depressed, chosen another career path. Not Hugh. He began by designing revolutionary prostheses enabling him not just to climb but to climb at a higher level than ever before. The new limbs carried special feet for ice climbing or difficult rockface scaling and allowed Hugh to alter his height for maximum efficiency and a greater range of hand and toeholds. With his designs attached, Hugh was an enhanced climber: a real bionic man.

Now, Herr designs bionic limbs that connect electrically to the wearer's nervous system: artificial body parts that can be controlled under neural impulse. And that's not all. Herr's Centre for Extreme Bionics, at Massachusetts' premier brainiac colony MIT, is developing prostheses with actual organic nerves in them, which link to the existing axons so well they can make the wearer feel like they still have genuine flesh and blood arms or legs.

These are prostheses that can dance, run, and jump. The Centre's most emblematic success story to date is a bespoke limb for ballroom dancer Adrianne Haslet-Davis, who lost a leg in 2013's Boston Marathon bomb attack, and whose return performance was given at a TED lecture delivered by Herr in March 2014.

'A human being can never be broken. Technology is broken. Technology is inadequate,' says Herr. Not anymore. The man with the plan is bringing better design to the human body."

This is an amazing story of a man who had every right to feel sorry for himself and to spend the rest of his life angry and asking himself 'why me?' But Herr is made of different stuff, with an overcoming and resilient spirit. Instead of seeing what he didn't have, he looked at what he did have and vowed to do something positive - the rest is history.

Thought for Today

You can choose how you respond to almost every adversity.

Today think about how you respond to negative things when they happen. You can choose how you respond to most things in life. You can give up or fight. If you fight, good things usually happen. The message is clear - Don't Give Up!

Today's Reflection

_____

_____

_____

_____

_____

_____

_____

_____

_____

_____

_____

_____

FROM BROKE TO BILLIONAIRE

*B*rian Acton was the software engineer that no one wanted to hire. Despite a dozen years of experience at Yahoo and Apple Computer, he got turned down by two of the internet's most upcoming companies at the time. First, Twitter, and then Facebook.

Jan Koum was a struggling businessman when he first moved to the US from the Ukraine, needing food stamps to survive. He had been raised in a rural community, in a house with no running hot water or electricity. Once settled in the US, he eventually got a job as an infrastructure engineer and worked at various companies, including Yahoo.

When he could not find any other company that would hire him, Acton teamed up with Koum and built the application that has not only dominated cloud-based messaging but is also used all over the world. These two people who had nothing going for them and no real future to look forward to developed WhatsApp!

WhatsApp was acquired by Facebook in 2014 for about $19 billion USD in cash and stock, making Acton's net worth around $3.8 billion. Apparently, Koum's worth in the deal, which is the largest acquisition by the Mark Zuckerberg-led firm, is even bigger than the amount Facebook offered Snapchat. Koum's deal was worth around $6.8 billion.

This is an excellent example of two people who were scraping a living and in Acton's case, not making a living, who created something out of nothing. What did they have that others didn't have? Was it a positive mindset? Was it creativity? Was it the willingness to go the extra mile? I know one thing for sure - this wouldn't have happened without a great deal of willpower, self-belief, and long hours.

Thought for Today

Even when things look extremely bleak, if you have faith and strong belief, good things can still happen.

Today think about your personal situation and areas where you may have given up. Look at these again and start to believe that success is still possible. As you do this, your faith will grow, and this, in turn, will increase your motivation and elevate your energy levels.

Today's Reflection

_____

_____

_____

_____

_____

_____

_____

_____

_____

_____

_____

_____

_____

POTATOES, EGGS, AND COFFEE BEAN.

'*O*nce upon a time, a daughter complained to her father that her life was miserable and that she didn't know how she was going to make it. She was tired of fighting and struggling all the time. It seemed just as one problem was solved, another one soon followed.*

Her father, a chef, took her to the kitchen. He filled three pots with water and placed each on a high fire. Once the three pots began to boil, he placed potatoes in one pot, eggs in the second pot, and ground coffee beans in the third pot. After twenty minutes, he turned off the burners. He took the potatoes out of the pot and placed them in a bowl. He pulled the eggs out and placed them in a bowl.

He then ladled the coffee out and placed it in a cup. Turning to her, he asked. "Daughter, what do you see?" "Potatoes, eggs, and coffee," she hastily replied. "Look closer," he said, "and touch the potatoes." She did and noted that they were soft. He then asked her to take an egg and break it. After pulling off the shell, she observed the hard-boiled egg. Finally, he asked her to sip the coffee. Its rich aroma brought a smile to her face.

"Father, what does this mean?" she asked. He then explained that the potatoes, the eggs, and coffee beans had each faced the same adversity– the boiling water. However, each one

reacted differently. The potato went in strong, hard, and unrelenting, but in boiling water, it became soft and weak.

The egg was fragile, with the thin outer shell protecting its liquid interior until it was put in the boiling water. Then the inside of the egg became hard. However, the ground coffee beans were unique. After they were exposed to the boiling water, they changed the water and created something new.

"Which are you," he asked his daughter. "When adversity knocks on your door, how do you respond? Are you a potato, an egg, or a coffee bean?"

Moral: In life, things happen around us, things happen to us, but the only thing that truly matters is what happens within us.'

Thought for Today

Which one are you? Egg, Potato, or Coffee Beans?

Today think how you respond to pressure - do you crumble, or do you improve in character and comfort zone? Remember, we only grow when we are under pressure. When things are going well, that is when we rest and recharge. If you embrace this fact, you will start to enjoy pressure situations knowing that you are growing and maturing.

Today's Reflection

_____

_____

_____

_____

_____

_____

_____

_____

_____

_____

_____

_____

_____

THE ANT AND THE GRASSHOPPER

*A*nts are small but smart. They store up food all summer. In the summertime, the ant is busy working, gathering food while the grasshopper plays. Then winter sets in, and the ant retires to his home and enjoys life. He paid the price; now, he can enjoy his reward. But now it's time for the grasshopper that played on the front end, to pay on the back end.

As a result, he starves in the cold because he didn't understand that the only adequate preparation for tomorrow is the wise use of today. Think about it; when you were at school, did you ever prepare for an exam so well that you knew as you walked in that you would pass that exam? Well, you can bring that same confidence to everyday life.

Sadly, most of us don't lead our lives; we accept them! But life's not a dress rehearsal. You don't get a second chance! Benjamin Disraeli said: 'The secret of success is to be ready when the opportunity comes.' Nothing great is created suddenly; success doesn't occur overnight. Neither does failure. Each is a process.

The fact is every day of your life is preparation for the next. The question is, what are you preparing for, and how are you preparing? Are you grooming yourself for success or failure? Only if you're willing to work hard on the front end, will you reap the rewards on the back end. I used to think that my skills alone would take me to the top, but I was sadly mistaken – hard work is the key.

Do you plan your days/weeks/months/years? There is much evidence to demonstrate that spending time planning saves you time and makes you more productive. By scheduling your most important tasks first, you will have the energy to complete them, and this will result in a feeling of achievement and progress.

By taking on and completing these, you are creating a successful future similar to the Ant. Ask yourself a simple question: Are you an Ant or a Grasshopper?

Thought for Today

Are you preparing yourself for success or failure in life?

Today think about the Ant and the Grasshopper - are you preparing for a wonderful future or a bleak future? The planning and work you put in today directly affects your future happiness. Don't sacrifice a beautiful future for some short-term pleasure and fun. The key is to have a healthy balance of work and fun.

Today's Reflection

_____

_____

_____

_____

_____

_____

_____

_____

_____

_____

_____

_____

WHAT YOU DO MAKES A DIFFERENCE!

The late Peter Marshall was an eloquent speaker and, for several years, served as the chaplain of the US Senate. He used to love to tell the story of the "Keeper of the Spring," a quiet forest dweller who lived high above an Austrian village along the eastern slope of the Alps.

The old gentleman had been hired many years earlier by a young town councilman to clear away the debris from the pools of water up in the mountain crevices that fed the lovely spring flowing through their town. With faithful, silent regularity, he patrolled the hills, removed the leaves and branches, and wiped away the silt that would otherwise have choked and contaminated the fresh flow of water.

The village soon became a popular attraction for vacationers. Graceful swans floated along the crystal-clear spring, the mill wheels of various businesses located near the water turned day and night, and the view from restaurants was picturesque beyond description.

Years passed. One evening the town council met for its semi-annual meeting. As they reviewed the budget, one man's eye caught the salary figure being paid to the obscure keeper of the spring. Said the keeper of the purse, "Who is the old man? Why do we keep him on year after year? No one ever sees him. For all we know, the strange ranger of the hills is doing us no good. He isn't necessary any longer." By a unanimous vote, they dispensed with the old man's services.

For several weeks, nothing changed.

By early autumn, the trees began to shed their leaves. Small branches snapped off and fell into the pools, hindering the rushing flow of sparkling water. One afternoon someone noticed a slight yellowish-brown tint in the spring. A few days later, the water was much darker. Within another week, a slimy film covered sections of the water along the banks, and a foul odour was soon detected. The mill wheels moved more slowly; some finally ground to a halt. Swans left, as did the tourists. Clammy fingers of disease and sickness reached deeply into the village.

Quickly, the embarrassed council called a special meeting. Realizing their gross error in judgment, they rehired the old keeper of the spring, and within a few weeks, the veritable river of life began to clear up. The wheels started to turn, and new life returned to the hamlet in the Alps.

Thought for Today

Do you sometimes wonder what impact you have in your role at work or home?

Remember what you do and say has a real impact, but you are probably not aware of it. Today think about the beautifully simple story of the 'Keeper of the Spring' and know that even though this man wasn't rewarded at the time, what he did made a huge difference. So just be happy knowing that your good deeds and words impact others in ways you will never believe.

Today's Reflection

_____
_____
_____
_____
_____
_____
_____
_____
_____
_____

Thomas A. Edison:

"Our greatest weakness lies in giving up. The most certain way to succeed is always to try just one more time."

A POSITIVE FROM A NEGATIVE

The name Art Fry may be unknown to you, but his invention has impacted the entire world with a product that is so well known, you will recognise it instantly.

The 3M Company encourages creativity from its employees. The company allows its researchers to spend 15 percent of their time on any project that interests them. This attitude has brought fantastic benefits not only to the employees but to the 3M Company itself. Many times, a spark of an idea turned into a successful product has boosted 3M's profits tremendously.

Some years ago, a scientist in 3M's commercial office took advantage of this 15 percent creative time. This scientist, Art Fry, came up with an idea for one of 3M's best-selling products. It seems that Art Fry dealt with a small irritation every Sunday as he sang in the church choir. After marking his pages in the hymnal with small bits of paper, the small pieces would invariably fall out all over the floor.

Suddenly, an idea struck Fry. He remembered an adhesive developed by a colleague that everyone thought was a failure because it did not stick very well. "I coated the adhesive on a paper sample," Fry recalls, "and I found that it was not only a good bookmark, but it was great for writing notes. It will stay in place as long as you want it to, and then you can remove it without damage."

Yes, Art Fry hit the jackpot. The resulting product was called Post-it! And has become one of 3M's most successful office products.

This suggests that 'out of every failure, there is a seed of an equal or greater benefit.' No matter what negative situation you find yourself in, I honestly believe that there is always the possibility of something positive hidden within it.

If you focus on the negative things in your world, you will feel negative, but if you focus on the positive things, you will feel more positive. When you are faced with something negative, always look for something positive in that situation. It may be something you can learn, or something which makes you stronger, or something which grows your comfort zone.

Thought for Today

In every negative situation, there is always a seed of something positive.

Today think about the failure of this glue, which wasn't strong enough for any apparent purpose. On the surface, it looked like a complete disaster, but it was the complete opposite. Art Fry spotted the potential in this apparent failure, and this has become one of the most successful products ever produced by 3M.

Today's Reflection

_____

_____

_____

_____

_____

_____

_____

_____

_____

_____

_____

ADVERSITY IS THE GRINDSTONE OF LIFE

A dversity is the grindstone of life. Intended to polish you up, adversity also has the ability to grind you down. The impact and ultimate result depend on what you do with the difficulties that come your way. Consider the phenomenal achievements of people experiencing adversity.

Beethoven composed his greatest works after becoming deaf. Sir Walter Raleigh wrote the History of the World during a thirteen-year imprisonment. If Columbus had turned back, no one could have blamed him, considering the constant adversity he endured. Of course, no one would have remembered him either.

Abraham Lincoln achieved greatness by his display of wisdom and character during the devastation of the Civil War. Luther translated the Bible while enduring confinement in the Castle of Wartburg. Under a sentence of death and during twenty years in exile, Dante wrote the Divine Comedy. John Bunyan wrote Pilgrim's Progress in a Bedford jail.

Finally, consider a more recent example. Mary Groda-Lewis endured sixteen years of illiteracy because of unrecognized dyslexia, was sent to a reformatory on two different occasions, and almost died of a stroke while bearing a child. Committed to going to college, she worked at a variety of odd jobs to save money, graduated with her high school equivalency at eighteen, was named Oregon's outstanding Upward Bound student, and finally entered college.

Determined to become a doctor, she faced fifteen medical school rejections until Albany Medical College finally accepted her. In 1984, Dr. Mary Groda-Lewis, at thirty-five, graduated with honors to fulfil her dream.

Adversity - the grindstone of life. Will it grind you down or polish you up?

I believe that the only time our character grows is when we are under pressure or facing adversity. When we are not under pressure is the time when we rest and recover. Rest and recovery are crucial to achieving a happy and well-balanced life. We need to rest our bodies and minds regularly, or we face burnout.

Thought for Today

Adversity - the grindstone of life. Will it grind you down or polish you up?

Today think about how you respond to pressure. Do you see it as just a painful process, or do you see it as a tough situation with an opportunity to grow? See if you can think of any situations you can view differently to embrace pressure.

Today's Reflection

_____

_____

_____

_____

_____

_____

_____

_____

_____

_____

_____

_____

DREAMS DO COME TRUE!

Julie and I flew to Dubai, where I delivered my Mental Resilience Masterclass to the staff of the British University in Dubai. On a previous visit to Dubai, I met with the Vice-Chancellor of the University Professor Abdullah. Following this meeting, we had many discussions, and we finally arrived at an agreement for me to deliver the Masterclass to his staff.

This was extremely exciting because this was the first time we had travelled to Dubai with guaranteed paid work. We had previously visited Dubai on three occasions with the goal of trying to establish some business there, and we finally achieved that.

Each time I visited Dubai, I could see the potential for business growth, but there was no guarantee that this would happen. I had to believe that this was possible, and my Dream Board helped me to believe. My Dream Board is basically a 'bucket list' of things I want to achieve and beautiful places I want to visit but in pictures rather than words. Pictures 'paint a thousand words,' and there seems to be more power in pictures than in words.

Just three short years ago, I was decorating to pay the bills before my business took off, I was in debt and working as a decorator on £80 a day. My future looked bleak, and I was on my own with very little to look forward to.

This is when I discovered the Dream Board the critical importance of maintaining a positive mindset in the worst of circumstances. I developed a series of techniques to help me stay positive most of the day, no matter what was happening in my life. By doing this, I noticed things turning around, so I carried on with more intensity. Every morning I spend about 20 minutes visualising the dreams on my board as if I have achieved each one.

My belief is that the feelings we experience daily are important to our future. If we can feel more positive than negative during the day, then we are winning and bringing good things to our future. Gratitude is a key, as is forgiveness.

Thought for Today

Revisit your Dream Board today.

Have you created a Dream Board yet? If not, take
some time this week to create one. Think of all
the wonderful places you would like to visit or
the people or charities you want to help. Maybe
you want to learn a new skill or learn how to play
an instrument. Perhaps you would like to meet
someone you really admire from a distance.

Today's Reflection

_____
_____
_____
_____
_____
_____
_____
_____
_____
_____
_____
_____

HE WAS PREPARED TO DIE

A young girl named Liz was suffering from a rare and serious disease. Her only chance of recovery was a blood transfusion from her five-year-old brother. He had miraculously survived the same disease and developed the antibodies needed to combat the illness.

The doctor explained the situation to her little brother and asked him if he would be willing to give his blood to his sister.

The boy hesitated for a moment before taking a deep breath and saying, "Yes. I'll do it if it will save her."

As the transfusion progressed, he lay in bed next to his sister and smiled as the colour returned to her cheeks. Then his face grew pale, and his smile faded. He looked up at the doctor and asked in a trembling voice, "Will I start to die right away?"

Being so young, the little boy had misunderstood; he thought he had to give his sister all of his blood to save her.

This is a powerful account of the sacrifice her little brother made, and it brought a tear to my eye. He was willing to die to save his sister which is staggering in its simplicity and amazing commitment. Her appreciation for what he did would have been huge, yet we don't have to make such big sacrifices to impact others and make a difference.

In the case of the little brother, he was willing to sacrifice his life for his sister. He would have thought long and hard over this decision, but he finally decided that doing the right thing was the most important thing. He had the power to save his sister, and he decided to take that opportunity at the expense of his own life.

Thinking about the needs of others is a wonderful way to feel better about yourself. You cannot help someone in any way at all and not benefit yourself as a result. Something happens when you do this, and it simply makes you feel good.

Thought for Today

What can you do today to make a difference?

Today think back to a time when you helped someone in some way and try to remember how that felt. Try to remember how this came about and how the person felt when you had helped them. Reflect on what it meant to them. It doesn't have to be much to make a big difference; sometimes, they just need to know someone cares.

Today's Reflection

_____

_____

_____

_____

_____

_____

_____

_____

_____

_____

_____

_____

_____

DAY 35

THE GOLD BOX

'A man punished his four-year-old daughter for wasting a roll of golden wrapping paper. Money was tight, and he became infuriated when the child used it to try to decorate a box to put under the Christmas tree.

Nevertheless, the little girl brought the gift to her father the next morning and said, "This is for you, Daddy."

The man was embarrassed by his earlier over-reaction, but his anger flared again when he found the box was empty. He yelled at his daughter, "Don't you know, when you give someone a present, there is supposed to be something inside?"

The little girl looked up at him with tears in her eyes and cried, "Oh Daddy, it's not empty at all. I blew kisses into the box. They're all for you, Daddy."

The father's anger was crushed. He put his arms around his little girl and begged for her forgiveness.

The father kept that box by his bed for many years. And, whenever he felt down, he took out an imaginary kiss and remembered the love of the child who had put it there.'

My eyes filled with tears when I read this, and I wondered how many times I have taken the small things for granted. The smile, the gentle touch on the arm, the hug, the kiss, the encouragement, the pat on the back. Often it is the small things in life which are the most precious, and it is important that we don't miss these in life.

It's not about the size of the house we own or how flashy the car we drive, but it's really about the people in our lives and our relationship with them. I have found that my true happiness lies in the people closest to me in life and the love we share.

Thought for Today

How are your relationships with the key people in your life?

Today think about all the key people in your life and see if there are any relationships which could do with a bit of attention. Do you need to apologise for something or treat someone to a night out? Do you need to spend a bit of quality time with someone or simply be a listening ear? Relationships play a key part in Mental Resilience.

Today's Reflection

_____

_____

_____

_____

_____

_____

_____

_____

_____

_____

_____

_____

THE POWER OF INTEGRITY

In 1994 golfer Davis Love called a one-stroke penalty on himself during the second round of the Western Open. He moved his marker out of the path of another player's putting line; then later he couldn't remember if he'd moved his ball back to its original spot. Since he wasn't certain, he gave himself an extra stroke.

And that one stroke caused him to be eliminated from the tournament. At the year's end, Love was $590 short in winnings to qualify for the Masters automatically and needed to win a tournament to get into one of golf's most coveted events.

Fortunately, the story ended well. The week before the big event, he qualified by winning a tournament in New Orleans and went on to earn $237,600 by finishing second in the 1995 Masters.

Later, when asked how he'd have felt if he'd missed the Masters because of calling a penalty on himself, Love replied, 'The question is how I'd have felt if I'd won and spent the rest of my life wondering if I'd cheated.'

What a great example of integrity – no one would have known apart from Davis alone if he had ignored that feeling he had inside. What I love about this story is that he was $590 short of qualifying, and by doing the right thing, he ended up winning $237,600. I don't believe that this was luck – the Law of Attraction comes to mind!

There is something incredibly special about living with integrity. There is a sense of peace and contentment about your life, even in the tougher times. Good things seem to happen when you do the right thing – eventually. It may take a long time, and it may seem as though nothing good has come from doing the right thing, but just wait and watch how your life starts to improve as you continue to do the right thing. The Law of 'Sow and Reap' comes into play, and you reap a good harvest from the good seed you have sown.

Thought for Today

Life will eventually reward you for doing the right thing!

When you are faced with a choice between right and wrong, choose right. Today be aware of every decision you make and see if it is based on integrity. Are you sometimes tempted to say, 'no one will notice' or 'it's only a small white lie'? But living a peaceful, happy life starts with living a life of integrity.

Today's Reflection

_____

_____

_____

_____

_____

_____

_____

_____

_____

_____

_____

AN IMPOSSIBLE ACHIEVEMENT

*T*he Brooklyn Bridge in the USA that spans the river tying Manhattan Island to Brooklyn is truly a miracle bridge. In 1863, a creative engineer named John Roebling was inspired by an idea for this spectacular bridge. However, bridge-building experts throughout the world told him to forget it; it could not be done.

Roebling convinced his son, Washington, who was a young up and coming engineer that the bridge could be built. The two of them developed the concepts of how it could be accomplished and how the obstacles could be overcome. With un-harnessed excitement and inspiration, they hired their crew and began to build their dream bridge.

The project was only a few months under construction when a tragic accident on the site took the life of John Roebling and severely injured his son, Washington. Washington was left with permanent brain damage and was unable to talk or walk.

Everyone felt that the project would have to be scrapped since the Roeblings were the only ones who knew how the bridge could be built. Even though Washington was unable to move or talk, his mind was as sharp as ever, and he still had a burning desire to complete the bridge.

An idea hit him as he lay in his hospital bed, and he developed a code for communication. All he could move was one finger, so he touched the arm of his wife with that finger, tapping out the code to communicate to her what to tell the engineers who were building the bridge.

For thirteen years, Washington tapped out his instructions with his finger until the spectacular Brooklyn Bridge was finally completed.

What a remarkable story! I don't know how this man had the ability to develop this communication system, which allowed him to oversee the building of the bridge. What I do know is that without his mental resilience and positive mindset, he wouldn't have even given it another thought.

He would have given up and been severely depressed, laying in his bed 24 hours a day knowing his dream was over. But that inner drive, the vision of the completed bridge which was burned into his subconscious mind, drove him to eventual success. He had achieved the near-impossible and would live the rest of his life, knowing he succeeded.

Thought for Today

You can choose how you respond to almost every situation.

Today ponder on the story of Washington and the amazing mindset which drove him to achieve the near impossible. This was a truly mind-boggling achievement with barely any movement in his body. Think about the challenges you currently have and see if there are any which you could dust off and try again.

Today's Reflection

_____

_____

_____

_____

_____

_____

_____

_____

_____

_____

_____

WATERSTONES BOOK SIGNING

The day finally arrived when I could set up the room on the fourth floor at Waterstones Nottingham for my long-awaited book launch. I experienced some very strange emotions that day, with many flashbacks to my early childhood days, where I failed very miserably at school.

I only came away with 3 GCE O Levels, and one of those was woodwork! I remember my mother coming to school to ask if I could stay on to sixth form, and the head teacher said **not a chance** as I had been a pupil who didn't study and was disruptive.

It was humiliating to experience my mother hearing these words from the head teacher, and I can only guess how she felt. But because she loved me so much, she didn't chastise me but encouraged me to go to college and study engineering. She demonstrated a love so deep that I didn't drop out, but she gave me the hope that one day I could make something of my life.

What really surprises me is that English was by far my worst subject in school, and I got the lowest grade possible when I took my O Level exam. I haven't studied English since the day I left school at the age of 16, and yet I find myself at my very own book signing. My book coach told me that my command of English is good, and she was confident for me to write the book with little input from her.

My experience in school was extremely negative, and sadly I didn't achieve the potential I could have achieved. But it is never too late to get things right, and over the past couple of years, in particular, I have turned things around, and I've found passion in my life again. Passion is key to many things in life because once you find a passion for something, it is very likely you will succeed. Passion drives you to go further than you would normally.

Only two years previously, I had been a full-time decorator. I know that it has been hard work, desire, application, and an attitude that I would never give up that has turned things around.

Thought for Today

It Is Not How You Start in Life Which Counts, But How You Finish.

Today think about your life and how you feel you have lived it. Are you happy where you are right now? Are there any areas you would like to improve? Finishing your life well is one of the great outcomes of good Mental Resilience. The wonderful news is that no matter what age you are right now, you can change where you are heading by changing the way you think, speak, and act.

Today's Reflection

_____
_____
_____
_____
_____
_____
_____
_____
_____
_____

NEVER GIVE UP!

A fter leaving school, he briefly considered joining the Indian Army and hiked in the Himalayan mountains of Sikkim and West Bengal. Eventually, he joined the Territorial Army and, after passing selection, served as a reservist with the SAS in 21 SAS Regiment (Artists) (Reserve), for three years until 1997.

In 1996, he suffered a free-fall parachuting accident in Zambia. His canopy ripped at 16,000 ft, partially opening, causing him to fall and land on his parachute pack on his back, which partially crushed three vertebrae.

He later said: "I should have cut the main parachute and gone to the reserve but thought there was time to resolve the problem." According to his surgeon, he came "within a whisker" of being paralyzed for life, and at first, it was questionable whether he would ever walk again. He spent the next 12 months in and out of military rehabilitation.

In a showcase of what pure determination and hard work can do, on 16 May 1998, he achieved his childhood dream and climbed to the summit of Mount Everest, 18 months after breaking three vertebrae in a parachuting accident.

At 23, he was at the time among the youngest people to have achieved this feat. This is the inspirational story of the amazing Bear Grylls. He is known to the world as a television presenter for the Discovery Channel, with his own show called Man Vs. Wild.

We often think that people who have made it have it easy in life and that things just fell in their lap. But the truth is that in 99% of cases, those very people have had to work extremely hard and have had to face many setbacks.

These setbacks can break people and often do. I wonder how many people have given up just before they were about to break through, or I wonder how many inventions have never come to market because people gave up too soon.

When things are tough, it is natural to want to give up. Everyone has doubts, everyone has times when they want to throw in the towel, but the people who finally succeed are the ones who don't stay in that negative place. They find a way to get themselves back up and think positively again.

Thought for Today

When you are positive, you have more energy

Today think about this statement and let it sink in.
It makes sense that when we have more energy,
we achieve more. When we achieve more, we feel
good and therefore have more energy, so we achieve
more, and the cycle goes on. On the contrary,
when we are negative, the opposite is true. Today
when you start thinking negatively, try to shift your
thinking onto something positive, and watch what
happens.

Today's Reflection

_____

_____

_____

_____

_____

_____

_____

_____

_____

_____

A RANDOM ACT OF KINDNESS

One night close to midnight in the 1960s, an older African-American woman was standing on the side of an Alabama highway in a lashing rainstorm.

Her car had broken down, and she desperately needed a ride. Soaking wet, she decided to flag down the next car. A young white man stopped to help her, which usually never happened at that place and time.

The young man took her to safety, helped her get assistance, and put her into a taxicab. She seemed to be in a big hurry but wrote down his address and thanked him.

Seven days went by, and a knock came on the young man's door. To his surprise, a giant console colour TV had been delivered to his home.

The note attached to it read:

"Thank you so much for assisting me on the highway the other night—the rain-drenched not only my clothes but also my spirits. Then you came along. Because of you, I was able to make it to my dying husband's bedside just before he passed away.

God bless you for helping me and unselfishly serving others. Sincerely, Mrs. Nat King Cole."

This is a lovely example of someone who decided to stop for someone in distress. It took the man some effort and inconvenience, but he chose to put that to one side and simply help someone in need. He didn't know that this lady happened to be the wife of the famous Nat King Cole.

His sacrifice meant that Mrs. Cole was able to hold her husband's hand as he slipped away, and this is priceless. This man then had the knowledge for the rest of his life that his random act of kindness really made a difference. The inner joy he experienced is beyond words and can only be obtained by helping someone.

Thought for Today

You never know who you are blessing when you help someone.

Today look for opportunities to help people no matter how small the gesture. You never know what they are going through, and you could be the one to bring them back from the brink or just make them smile. It doesn't cost anything, but it can make a huge difference to someone's day. The next time you see an opportunity to help someone, take it.

Today's Reflection

_____
_____
_____
_____
_____
_____
_____
_____
_____
_____

Eleanor Roosevelt:

"The future belongs to those who believe in the beauty of their dreams."

LEARN TO BOUNCE BACK

*B*efore he became the legend that he is today, Walt Disney was struggling to make ends meet. In 1919 he was fired by the editor of the newspaper he was working for, as he "lacked imagination and had no good ideas"!

In January 1920, Walt formed a short-lived company with a fellow cartoonist; however, this did not bring the financial stability that was needed and so Walt temporarily left, to enable him to earn money at the Kansas City Film Ad Company.

He eventually managed to acquire his own studio, and whilst it achieved moderate success, the profits were insufficient to cover the high salaries paid to the employees, leaving the studio loaded with debt and with no alternative other than to declare the company bankrupt.

Undeterred, he decided to set up a studio in the movie industry's capital city, Hollywood, California. He created Oswald the Lucky Rabbit, which was one of his first successes in the cartooning business. At the time, though, he was only receiving a 20 percent cut on his films and was ready to negotiate better terms since he was barely making a living.

He experienced another setback when his producer stole the character, along with the production crew, with whom he'd negotiated new contracts. His producer thought he would give in and accept the mere 20% he was paid.

Whilst many people would pack their bags and return home defeated, or accept working for the minimum wage, this dauntless young man did neither and subsequently went on to create his most successful cartoon character ever – Mickey Mouse.

Walt Disney was an entrepreneur, cartoonist, animator, voice actor, and film producer. He did not let a string of failures overcome him, continually believing in his true worth, standing strong even through his toughest times. There must not be a single person who does not know Disney or hasn't heard the name Disney.

The newspaper editor who fired him for a "lack of imagination and no good ideas" must have been kicking himself for having let go, the founder of, arguably, the most imaginative company in the world.

Walt Disney had a lot of setbacks during his life, but his positive mindset kept him moving forward, bouncing back from every setback. I have observed that all high achievers have the ability to be knocked down and get back up again. They don't stay down for long.

Thought for Today

How good are you at bouncing back when you are faced with adversity?

Today think about times in your life when things have gone wrong and try to remember how you responded. Did you fight back and try again, or did you give up? Sometimes we need to know when to give up, but most times, it is good to try again. If we keep bouncing back, we will often find success at the end of that road.

Today's Reflection

_____

_____

_____

_____

_____

_____

_____

_____

_____

_____

_____

IT'S HOW YOU RESPOND

"*Nicolo Paganini was a well-known and gifted nineteenth-century violinist. He was also well known as a great showman with a quick sense of humour. His most memorable concert was in Italy with a full orchestra. He was performing before a packed house, and his technique was incredible; his tone was fantastic, and his audience dearly loved him.*

Toward the end of his concert, Paganini was astounding his audience with an unbelievable composition when suddenly one string on his violin snapped and hung limply from his instrument. Paganini frowned briefly, shook his head, and continued to play, improvising beautifully.

Then, to everyone's surprise, a second string broke. And shortly thereafter, a third. Almost like a slapstick comedy, Paganini stood there with three strings dangling from his Stradivarius. But instead of leaving the stage, Paganini stood his ground and calmly completed the difficult number on the one remaining string."

Paganini demonstrated how to respond to adversity in front of a live audience. We can all choose how we respond to almost every situation we face. What we focus on effects how we feel. If we focus on the positive, we feel better; if we focus on the negative, we feel worse.

This brings back a memory from a couple of years ago when I was speaking on a Cruise Liner in the Caribbean. I was halfway through my presentation when my laptop shut down. I didn't know what was happening, so as the technician came running down from the sound desk to sort the problem out, I started telling some stories from my basketball days.

I had forgotten to plug my charger in, and it had run out of battery. He found the charger, plugged it in and the laptop fired up. Then to my horror, Windows Update popped up and started to install. This meant I had to continue telling stories, and as I finished my very last story, the laptop came to life.

I could have frozen on the spot and looked embarrassed, but my Mindset and Mental Resilience meant that I performed well under pressure.

Thought for Today

How do you respond when something goes badly wrong?

Today think about your usual response to things going wrong in your life. How do you respond? Do you crumble under pressure, or do you keep calm and carry on? To perform well under pressure, you need a positive inner voice, and this is something you can develop. Feel free to email me at john@ jdmindcoach.com to receive a free copy of the Inner Voice Worksheet to develop your own positive inner voice

Today's Reflection

_____

_____

_____

_____

_____

_____

_____

_____

_____

_____

THIS IS WHY I DO WHAT I DO

A couple of weeks ago, I received this email from a school head of year, and the contents of this brought a tear to my eye. I have removed any names to keep this confidential.

Good morning John.

I am sorry that it has taken time for me to respond to you. I was really impressed with your presentation to the students at our school. You were a breath of fresh air at a time they were feeling tired and stressed about their upcoming exams. The students felt that their exams went well, and they were all in good spirits for their Prom.

However, your presentation also had an impact on me. I have thought about and used some of your techniques in my role as Head of Year. I am also in the process of reading your book. I find each chapter inspiring and extremely helpful.

The other evening, I had to deliver a presentation at a parent's assembly. I took on board some of your advice and had the presentation planned and practiced (and changed several times) a week before the evening.

As an introvert, I expel a great deal of energy when I present, which can leave me very tired afterwards.

I also get very nervous as well. However, I thought about some of the key phrases you use, in particular 'I am going to enjoy this' and 'I am excited.' I thought this is a great opportunity to go out there and enjoy it. I really did enjoy it, and it was a great success. The parents were engaged and thanked me on their way out.

In the past, I have had similar evenings, but it felt different this time. I felt confident, and I felt good afterwards.

This makes it all worthwhile. It just confirms that the techniques I teach are simple but very effective in changing thinking, speaking, and ultimately actions. You need to create a positive inner voice with some key phrases which you can repeat over and over again whenever you feel nervous. As you do this, you will feel negative thoughts and anxiety leave your mind, and you will perform better.

I have a full chapter on this in my first book 'Off the Wall – How to develop World Class Mental Resilience' with details at the end of this book.

Thought for Today

Do you sometimes wonder if what you do is making a difference?

If you do, then maybe, it's just that you haven't had the feedback yet. Today think back to any times in your life when someone has thanked you for something you have done. Keep thinking about this and see what memories you can bring back. These were times when you were appreciated, and you made a difference. Don't stop helping people as the impact is the same whether you receive thanks or not.

Today's Reflection

_____

_____

_____

_____

_____

_____

_____

_____

_____

VISUALISE THE FUTURE YOU WANT

There is power in visualisation; it does something to your mind and your energy levels.

Many successful people swear by this, including famous people like Oprah Winfrey, Arnold Schwarzenegger, Will Smith, and Jim Carrey. They put down their success to visualising the future they want, keeping a positive mindset, and working hard.

Arnold Schwarzenegger
As a child, he picked up a magazine with Mr. Universe, Reg Park, on the cover as the star of the new movie, Hercules. As Arnold read through the magazine, the whole plan began to unfold for him. He was going to follow Reg Park's footsteps, become a bodybuilding champion and a huge movie star.

To his family and friends, this idea was incredibly...stupid. Bodybuilding was not a big thing back then – especially in a little Austrian village. But, despite their disbelief, Arnold began training like a mad man, always keeping his vision in mind.

Arnold Schwarzenegger swore by the power of visualization to reach his bodybuilding goals.

"I had this fixed idea of growing a body like Reg Park's. The model was there in my mind; I only had to grow enough to fill it," he explained. "The more I focused in on this image and worked and grew, the more I saw it was real and possible for me to be like him."

Later, when he transitioned to careers in acting and politics, Schwarzenegger said he employed similar mental tricks: "It's the same process I used in bodybuilding: What you do is create a vision of who you want to be — and then live that picture as if it were already true."

There is amazing power in visualisation. I have used these techniques for the past few years, and my entire life has transformed. Amazing things have appeared in my life, and I am now a published author and international speaker. You need to have a vision of who you want to become or what you want to achieve to fulfil your potential. A clear picture of where you want to go drives you further than you would ever go without that vision.

As motivational speaker Zig Ziglar once said, "How can you hit a target you don't have?"

Thought for Today

If your vision is strong enough, it will drive you to success.

Do you have a clear vision of what you want to achieve in life? Today think about your goals and dreams, and if they are clear and written down, well done! If they are not clear and written down, then I suggest you spend some time visualising the future you desire and what you want that to look like. You will then start to see these things start to appear in your life.

Today's Reflection

_____

_____

_____

_____

_____

_____

_____

_____

_____

_____

IT'S NOT HOW YOU START BUT HOW YOU FINISH!

"An elderly carpenter was ready to retire. He told his employer/contractor of his plans to leave the house-building business and live a more leisurely life with his wife enjoying his extended family. He would miss the paycheck, but he needed to retire. They could get by.

The contractor was sorry to see his good worker go and asked if he could build just one more house as a personal favour. The carpenter said yes, but in time it was easy to see that his heart was not in his work. He resorted to shoddy workmanship and used inferior materials. It was an unfortunate way to end his career.

When the carpenter finished his work, and the builder came to inspect the house, the contractor handed the front-door key to the carpenter. "This is your house," he said, "my gift to you."

What a shock! What a shame! If he had only known he was building his own house, he would have done it all so differently. Now he had to live in the home he had built none too well."

It's not how you start in life, which counts, but how you finish. People don't remember the early parts of your life as much as they do in the latter years. I am determined to finish my life well, so I don't have any regrets.

I want to leave this world, feeling that I gave it everything I had and enjoyed the journey. I believe that when you find your passion, life is exciting and challenging, but it's also fun.

The statistics are shocking regarding how long people live after retirement when they don't have anything to look forward to. Those who do have like a hobby, an interest, or a cause to support, live far longer than those who don't.

Thought for Today

It's not how you start in life, which counts, but how you finish.

Today think about the standards you keep and how you finish things off. Do you consistently give your best, or do you sometimes allow lower levels of professionalism?
If you do not have job satisfaction, is there a cause you can get involved with? When you have passion for something, you give it your best.

Today's Reflection

_____

_____

_____

_____

_____

_____

_____

_____

_____

_____

FROM RAGS TO RICHES

*"**A**ndrew Carnegie was born in this small house in Dunfermline, Scotland, in 1835. For generations, the Carnegies had been master handloom weavers. But as the industrial revolution introduced steam-powered looms, the family business collapsed.*

Carnegie's family became so poor they'd go to sleep early to "forget the misery of hunger." He later wrote, "It was burnt into my heart then that my father had to beg (for work). And then and there came the resolve that I would cure that when I got to be a man."

At age 12, Carnegie moved with his family to Pittsburgh, where his two aunts lived. All of them slept in one room.

At 13, Carnegie started working in the boiler room of a textile factory. At night he had nightmares about the boiler exploding.

At age 17, Carnegie took a job as a telegrapher and assistant to a local railroad man for an impressive salary of $35 a month. Over the next decade, he became essential to running the profitable railroad.

Carnegie also started investing. A $217 investment in a sleeping car company soon paid $5,000 a year. He helped *form a pig iron company to build railroad bridges. His investments became so profitable that his $2400 a year from the railroad amounted to only 5 percent of his income.*

In 1865, Carnegie left the railroad and moved to New York, where he and his mother took a suite at the fashionable St Nicholas hotel.

In 1901, Carnegie, 66, sold his steel company to JP Morgan for $480 million, half of which went to Carnegie.

"The man who dies rich dies disgraced." Living by this motto, Carnegie devoted the last 18 years of his life to philanthropy. He donated to nearly 3,000 libraries, parks, education, arts, and world peace. He said candidly of philanthropy, "and besides, it provides a refuge from self-questioning."

What a great way to live and give.

This is a wonderful finish to this great story. Carnegie didn't retire and keep the fortune he had made. Instead, he changed the lives of millions by using that money to make a huge difference.

What an amazing way to live and what joy he would have received in those last 18 years by giving away all of his money, knowing that he was helping so many people. From rags to riches and from power to peace.

Thought for Today

Giving something back is a wonderful road to fulfilment and peace.

Today think about Andrew Carnegie and his journey from rags to riches. He died a very happy and fulfilled man knowing that he had made a huge difference to millions of people. What can you do now or in the future to help others in some way? This is a wonderful way to live a peaceful, fulfilled, and happy life. Is there someone you can think of now?

Today's Reflection

_____

_____

_____

_____

_____

_____

_____

_____

_____

_____

DAY 47

IF I HAD MY LIFE OVER

If I had my life to live over, I'd dare to make more mistakes next time.

I'd relax, I'd limber up.

I would be sillier than I've been this trip.

I would take fewer things seriously, take more chances, take more trips.

I'd climb more mountains, and swim more rivers.

I would eat more ice cream and less beans.

I would perhaps have more actual troubles, but I'd have fewer imaginary ones.

You see, I'm one of those people who lived seriously, sanely, hour after hour, day after day.

Oh, I've had my moments, and if I had it to do over again, I'd have more of them.

I've been one of those persons who never goes anywhere without a thermometer, a hot-water bottle, a raincoat, and a parachute.

If I had to do it again, I would travel lighter than this trip.

If I had my life to live over, I would start going barefoot earlier in the spring and stay that way later in the fall. I would go to more dances; I would ride more merry-go-rounds. I would pick more daisies.

I encourage people I work with to live a rich life. To smell the coffee and the roses. To experience things they haven't before. To take a risk or two to see what they can achieve and what they become during the process. Because it's what we become, that is the most exciting part.

To be aware of their surroundings several times during the day. To be in the present, fully aware of the beauty around them. Generally, we are so busy that we don't stop for a few moments just to appreciate the sunset, the beautiful meadow, or the lovely old couple holding hands.

To really live.

Thought for Today

Do you ever simply stop for a minute and take in your surroundings?

There is amazing beauty around us, but we just miss it because we are too busy. What can you find in your surroundings today? Take time today to take in the golden moments around you. As you do this, you cannot be stressed; you are simply in the moment, non-judgmentally. Do this many times a day to relax and de-stress.

Today's Reflection

_____

_____

_____

_____

_____

_____

_____

_____

_____

_____

_____

DREAM BOARD

Six years ago, I created a Dream Board, which was a list of things I wanted to achieve, and these dreams were represented by pictures.

One of the pictures on my board was a row of wooden bookcases in Waterstones representing the writing and publishing of my first book, a dream I'd had for many years, but kept putting off.

Every morning before starting work, I would spend about 30 minutes reading motivational books and visualising my dreams to put me in a positive state of mind for the day. I found that I achieved a great deal more in the day if I was positive and motivated.

After a short period of reading a motivational book, I would visualise actually achieving the things I have on my Dream Board. I would imagine myself in the future situation, having achieved the dream. I would do this in detail using all my senses and emotions to experience the achievement. By doing this, I experienced a new level of motivation.

Not long after intense visualisation of the book launch, I met Gail Powell, a book coach, and publisher, and had a half-day one-to-one session with her. This was far more than a coincidence, and I believe my consistent visualisation brought focus and strong desire, which connected us together.

Gail came up with an excellent title for the book, the audience I should be aiming for, even a really clever cover design. She thought my book idea was excellent, and as a result, I signed up with her and published my first book four years ago. You won't be surprised that she is publishing this book too!

Would this have all happened if I hadn't visualised Waterstones and a queue of people lining up for me to sign my book – I don't think so! She also had contact with Waterstones and told me that she could help to organise a book signing in Waterstones Nottingham, which all happened.

It still amazes me that at the age of 66, my life is exploding. I've found my passion in life, which is speaking, training, and coaching people to achieve more in their lives. I believe that part of this success is my constant positive mindset and giving out positive emotions and, of course visualising the future I desire. My 14-year plan to be speaking on stage at the age of 80 is alive and well.

Thought for Today

Create your own Dream Board.

Write a bucket list of things you want to achieve in your lifetime. Where do you want to travel to, what do you want to own, who do you want to help? Find pictures on Google which represent each one and copy and paste these onto an A4 document. Reduce each one and repeat until you have a Dream Board. Print this off and look at it every day.

Today's Reflection

_____

_____

_____

_____

_____

_____

_____

_____

_____

_____

_____

_____

THE WHOLE WORLD CAME TOGETHER

*T*he young mother was ready for a few minutes of
relaxation after a long and demanding day. However, her
young daughter had other plans for her mother's time.

"Read me a story, Mom," the little girl requested. "Give
Mommy a few minutes to relax and unwind. Then I'll be
happy to read you a story," pleaded the mother.

The little girl was insistent that Mommy read to her now.
With a stroke of genius, the mother tore off the back page
of the magazine she was reading. It contained a full-page
picture of the world.

As she tore it into several pieces, Mom asked her daughter to
put the picture together, and then she would read her a story.
Surely this would buy her considerable relaxing moments. A
short time later, the little girl announced the completion of
her puzzle project.

To her astonishment, she found the world picture completely
assembled. When she asked her daughter how she managed
to do it so quickly, the little girl explained that on the reverse
side of the page was the picture of a little girl. "You see,
Mommy, when I got the little girl together, the whole world
came together."

Each of us has the responsibility to put our world together. It starts by getting ourselves put together. We can become better parents, friends, spouses, employees, and employers. The first step is changing our attitude.

As we put ourselves together, we can impact others in a positive way. As we take care of our health and minds, we become more able to help others, and this, in turn, allows them to help others. It all starts with sorting ourselves out first. We need to become Mentally Resilient to help others.

Much like the situation on an aeroplane when the oxygen pressure in the cabin drops too low, the oxygen masks drop from above. If an adult is with a child, they are told to put the mask on first, but everything in them wants to put the mask on their helpless child.

It goes against our natural instincts, but if we were to do that in an emergency, it is possible that we could run out of air before we get the chance to put our own mask on, resulting in disaster.

In the same way, if we look after ourselves first, we can help others.

Thought for Today

You need to look after yourself first to help others.

Today think about what you are doing to look after your mental and physical health. Are you doing enough, or do you need to do more? What can you start doing tomorrow, which will make a difference? Try to think of one thing you can do, which will make you stronger, either mentally or physically.

Today's Reflection

_____

_____

_____

_____

_____

_____

_____

_____

_____

_____

_____

_____

SPEAK POSITIVE WORDS

"*Two men who shared a hospital room ended up becoming friends. One was allowed to sit up for an hour every day. His bed was beside the only window. The other man spent his life flat on his back. Each day the man at the window would describe the activity and colour of the outside world.*

The park overlooking the lake, ducks swimming, children playing, couples walking hand in hand, the skyline in the distance. His friend, who could see none of this, smiled and imagined it all in his mind's eye.

One day the man by the window died, and his roommate moved to his place. He propped himself up to look outside and was amazed to see a drab brick wall! Confused, he asked the nurse how come his friend had described the scenery in such glowing terms. She replied, 'Actually he was blind, and he couldn't even see the wall. He just wanted to encourage you.'

One author writes: 'When you tell somebody they are beautiful you change the way they see themselves. When a teacher tells a student they are smart, they work harder and achieve more. When a parent tells a child they are loved, they have the confidence to reach for the stars.

On the other hand, a doctor who point-blank tells a patient they are 'terminal' can speed up the death process. Words are powerful, use yours to build people up."

This is a potent message and can change lives once people understand the power of words. I have just been reading a book, and in it, the author proclaimed the following:

Change your words and change your life

The power of the tongue is remarkable. It can start wars, or it can heal a broken heart. It can destroy someone, or it can build someone. It can bring death or bring peace. It can break a marriage, or it can build a marriage. It can create distance, or it can create closeness.

In the same way, choose the words you say to yourself very carefully. What you say to yourself on a daily basis determines your future. Change your words and change your life.

Thought for Today

When you lift someone – you yourself are lifted.

Today think about the words you speak to others. See if you can increase the number of positive things you say during the day and observe how you feel. The great thing is that when you lift someone – you yourself are encouraged. How many people can you speak to today to restore their spirits? See it as a game to see how many positive things you can say.

Today's Reflection

_____

_____

_____

_____

_____

_____

_____

_____

_____

_____

_____

_____

George Eliot:

"It is never too late to be what you might have been."

TWO APPLES

"A *father and his daughter were playing in the park. His young daughter spotted an apple vendor. She asked her father to buy her an apple. The father didn't bring much money with him, but it was enough to purchase two apples. So, he bought two apples and gave them to his daughter.*

His daughter held one apple each in her two hands. Then the father asked her if she can share one apple with him. Upon hearing this, his daughter quickly took a bite from one apple, and before her father could speak, she also took a bite from the second apple.

Father was surprised. He wondered what mistake he made raising his daughter that she acted in such a greedy way. His mind was lost in thoughts, that perhaps he is just thinking too much, his daughter is too young to understand about sharing and giving. The smile had disappeared from his face.

Then suddenly his daughter, with an apple in her one hand, said, "Father have this one, this one is much juicier and sweeter." Her father was speechless. He felt bad about reaching to the judgement so quickly about a small child.

His smile came back now, knowing why his daughter quickly took a bite from each apple."

Don't judge too quickly

It is so easy for us to judge too quickly sometimes as the good intentions of people are often hidden or not obvious. This is a wonderful example of love in action. This is pure and without desire for anything in return. The objective was to make the other person happy – that was it. There was no hidden agenda, no hope for something in return; it was simply an act of kindness which brought joy to the other person once they realised what had happened.

Thought for Today

A couple of things to think about today. Firstly, in the past, have you judged someone's intentions too quickly, and secondly, can you think of any time in the past when you have performed an act of kindness for someone? What did it feel like? Did it make them feel good? This week see if you can act on either of these two areas.

Today's Reflection

_____

_____

_____

_____

_____

_____

_____

_____

_____

_____

_____

_____

_____

MOMENTUM IS THE KEY!

The book 'From Good to Great' mentions a very large flywheel, which is huge and very heavy. It is positioned horizontally, and author Jim Collins describes how starting to move this huge heavy flywheel is very difficult at the beginning, but eventually, breakthrough comes.

"Picture a huge, heavy flywheel—a massive metal disk mounted horizontally on an axle, about 30 feet in diameter, 2 feet thick, and weighing about 5,000 pounds. Now imagine that your task is to get the flywheel rotating on the axle as fast and long as possible.

Pushing with great effort, you get the flywheel to inch forward, moving almost imperceptibly at first. You keep pushing and, after two or three hours of persistent effort, you get the flywheel to complete one entire turn.

You keep pushing, and the flywheel begins to move a bit faster, and with continued great effort, you move it around a second rotation. You keep pushing in a consistent direction.

Three turns ... four ... five ... six ... the flywheel builds up speed ... seven ... eight ... you keep pushing ... nine ... ten ... it builds momentum ... eleven ... twelve ... moving faster with each turn ... twenty ... thirty ... fifty ... a hundred.

Then, at some point—breakthrough! The momentum of the thing kicks in your favour, hurling the flywheel forward, turn after turn ... whoosh! ... its own heavy weight working for you. You're pushing no harder than during the first rotation, but the flywheel goes faster and faster.

Each turn of the flywheel builds upon work done earlier, compounding your investment of effort. A thousand times faster, then ten thousand, then a hundred thousand. The huge heavy disk flies forward, with almost unstoppable momentum."

This is an exciting concept as it describes reaping the benefit of consistent hard work. There is no shortcut to good old-fashioned hard work. All happy high achievers in business, sport, music and the arts work incredibly hard to achieve success. So, the hard work is a given, but the rewards of this hard work are unbelievable.

You get to live the life you have dreamed of, and you are in a position to help others achieve their dreams.

Thought for Today

Have a dream, put the hard work in consistently, don't give up and then – 'One day, life will tap you on the shoulder and tell you it's your time.'

Today think about the message that hard work is a given. Do you accept that to achieve what you want in life takes hard work and some sacrifices? People who go to the gym know that it takes time and effort to achieve the results they want. Similarly, what you desire takes time and effort. What can you apply more patience to?

Today's Reflection

_____

_____

_____

_____

_____

_____

_____

_____

_____

REAP WHAT YOU SOW

I came across this story of Shania Twain, which is very inspirational because she thought of others first, and by doing so, she was rewarded –

"Twain's career began more out of necessity than raw ambition. Her parents divorced when she was two, and she rarely saw her father. Her mom and stepfather, to whom she grew close, often couldn't make enough to get by, so Twain started singing in bars to make extra money when she was just eight years old.

She recalls her mother waking her up at all hours to get up and perform. Sadly, when she was 21, her mother and stepfather were killed in a head-on car accident with a logging truck on the highway.

Twain put her career on hold to step in and take care of her three younger siblings (who were in their teens at the time). She sang in resorts and postponed going after big-time stardom until her sister and brothers were old enough to take care of themselves.

Only once her youngest brother graduated high school did she feel okay about heading down to Nashville to pursue her career."

Shania Twain, born Eilleen Regina Edwards; August 28, 1965, is a Canadian singer and songwriter. She has sold over 100 million records, making her the best-selling female artist in country music history and among the best-selling music artists of all time.

She has received five Grammy Awards, 27 BMI Songwriter Awards, she has stars on both Canada's Walk of Fame and the Hollywood Walk of Fame, and an induction into the Canadian Music Hall of Fame. She is the only female artist in history to have three consecutive albums certified Diamond by the RIAA.

Shania's story demonstrates that if you do the right things in life, it can all work out in the end. I love the fact that she thought about her siblings rather than herself, and by doing that, it all came good in the end.

Thought for Today

When you put others first, you will be blessed.

Today think about the sacrifice Shania Twain made to look after her siblings. She put her singing career on hold to care for them. But that wasn't the end of the story as life has a way of paying back good deeds. When she went to Nashville, opportunities opened up because what you sow is what you reap. Think of someone you can contact to ask if you can help with anything and see if you can make a difference to someone's life.

Today's Reflection

_____

_____

_____

_____

_____

_____

_____

_____

_____

_____

SHAKE OFF YOUR PROBLEMS

There was an old farmer whose donkey fell into an empty well. The farmer was old and the donkey was too. The farmer knew he didn't have enough strength to pull the donkey out of the deep hole. So he reasoned to himself, "This donkey is old. I am too. I can't get him out of this mess. It is better for the donkey and for me if I just bury him here in this hole.

He's had a good life and served me well, but I can't do anything with him now. It is better to bury him and put him out of his misery." So the farmer grabbed a shovel and started throwing in dirt.

The farmer could hear the donkey's cries from below. The donkey cried louder and louder with each pile of dirt, he threw. And then the cries stopped. The farmer felt relieved. He didn't want the donkey to suffer and was glad he was no longer in pain. "This is for the best," the farmer reasoned. He continued to fill up the hole.

However, the donkey decided to shake off the dirt and not let it affect him. Something amazing happened. When he shook off the dirt, it no longer affected him the same way. The dirt fell down around him. He used the dirt to STEP UP and GET UP on top of it.

STOP. SHAKE OFF. STEP UP. He did it over and over again. With every step he got stronger and more determined. The more dirt he shook off, the better he got at not letting it affect him.

The farmer couldn't believe his eyes. Instead of being dead, the donkey was very much alive. With every pile of dirt he was getting closer and closer to the surface. The farmer mistook his silence as a sign he had given up. The farmer had underestimated the donkey. If the donkey had just stood there and done nothing; he would have surely died.

The lesson behind this is that no matter what people say about you, do to try to harm you or tarnish your name, choose not to allow it to affect you but shake it off and begin to rise above it.

Thought for Today

How do you respond to problems?

When you are under a lot of pressure, how do
you respond? Today think about your response to
negative situations. Do you crumble under pressure,
or do you take on the challenge? How you respond
to any given situation determines the outcome. If
you take a positive 'Can Do' approach, the outcome
will always be better.

Today's Reflection

_____

_____

_____

_____

_____

_____

_____

_____

_____

_____

_____

_____

PATIENCE FOR THE LONG HAUL

"In the Far East, there is a tree called the Chinese bamboo tree. This remarkable tree is different from most trees in that it doesn't grow in the usual fashion. While most trees grow steadily over a period of years, the Chinese bamboo tree doesn't break through the ground for the first four years.

Then, in the fifth year, an amazing thing happens – the tree begins to grow at an astonishing rate. In fact, in a period of just five weeks, a Chinese bamboo tree can grow to a height of 90 feet. It's almost as if you can actually see the tree growing before your very eyes."

I'm convinced that life often works in a similar way. You can work for weeks, months, and even years on your dream with no visible signs of progress, and then, all of a sudden, things take off. Your business becomes profitable beyond your wildest dreams. Your marriage becomes more vibrant and passionate than you ever thought it could be.

Yet, all of this requires one thing – faith. The growers of the Chinese bamboo tree have faith that if they keep watering and fertilizing the ground, the tree will breakthrough. Well, you must have the same kind of faith in your bamboo tree, whether it is to run a successful business, win a Pulitzer Prize, or raise well-adjusted children.

Sadly, what many fail to realise is that pursuing a dream is a sure thing if you just don't give up. So long as you keep watering and fertilizing your dream, it will come to fruition. It may take weeks. It may take months. It may even take years, but eventually, the roots will take hold, and your tree will grow. And when it does, it will grow in remarkable ways.

We've seen this happen so many times. Henry Ford had to water his bamboo tree through five business failures before he finally succeeded with the Ford Motor Company. Richard Hooker had to water his bamboo tree for seven years and through 21 rejections by publishers until his humorous war novel, M*A*S*H, became a runaway bestseller, spawning a movie and one of the longest-running television series of all-time.

Thought for Today

Are you working hard but not seeing the results you want?

Don't despair; if you are working on the right things, you will breakthrough if you just keep going long enough. Today think about something you are working on and relate it to the bamboo. It may take longer than you want, but if you believe it is on its way, it will give you comfort and will reduce your stress. What is causing you frustration at the moment?

Today's Reflection

_____

_____

_____

_____

_____

_____

_____

_____

_____

A SPECIAL BANK ACCOUNT

I recently came across this story from America, which talks about our use of time and how easy it is to lose precious time every day.

"Imagine you had a bank account that deposited $86,400 each morning. The account carries over no balance from day to day, allows you to keep no cash balance, and every evening cancels whatever part of the amount you had failed to use during the day.

What would you do? Draw out every dollar each day! We all have such a bank. Its name is 'Time.' Every morning, it credits you with 86,400 seconds. Every night it writes off, as lost, whatever time you have failed to use wisely. It carries over no balance from day-to-day.

It allows no overdraft, so you can't borrow against yourself or use more time than you have. Each day, the account starts fresh. Each night, it destroys all unused time. If you fail to use the day's deposits, it's your loss, and you can't appeal to get it back.

There is never any borrowing time. You can't take a loan out on your time or against someone else's. The time you have is the time you have, and that is that. Time management is yours to decide how you spend the time, just as with money you decide how you spend the money.

It is never the case of us not having enough time to do things, but the case of whether we want to do them and where they fall in our priorities."

Laser-Like Focus

Good time management is key to this, and prioritising the important things you need to do each day is critical.

Don't let yourself just do the easy things all day long and still have those important tough things left to do. Do the tough things first thing – and do them in the morning when it has been proven we all have more energy. Yes, even the night birds who prefer to stay up late and get up a bit later.

We all have more energy in the morning and early afternoon – after that, we start to tail off. So, it makes sense to use your energy in the morning to tackle the tough things on your list. This is one of the key things to success.

Thought for Today

Good time management is the key to success.

Do you get the important things done each day? Research indicates that we have more energy between 6am and 1pm. Try to plan your hardest tasks during these times. The tasks which cause you to procrastinate lose their power when you have high energy. Schedule your complicated proposals, tough phone calls, and difficult meetings early.

Today's Reflection

_____

_____

_____

_____

_____

_____

_____

_____

_____

_____

_____

THE OBSTACLE IN OUR PATH

"There once was a very wealthy and curious king. This king had a huge boulder placed in the middle of a road. Then he hid nearby to see if anyone would try to remove the gigantic rock from the road.

The first people to pass by were some of the king's wealthiest merchants and courtiers. Rather than moving it, they simply walked around it. A few loudly blamed the King for not maintaining the roads. Not one of them tried to move the boulder.

Finally, a peasant came along. His arms were full of vegetables. When he got near the boulder, rather than simply walking around it as the others had, the peasant put down his load and tried to move the stone to the side of the road. It took a lot of effort, but he finally succeeded.

The peasant gathered up his load and was ready to go on his way when he saw a purse lying in the road where the boulder had been. The peasant opened the purse. The purse was stuffed full of gold coins and a note from the king. The king's note said the purse's gold was a reward for moving the boulder from the road.

The king showed the peasant what many of us never understand: every obstacle presents an opportunity to improve our condition."

This quote from Napoleon Hill is something I have lived and believed for many years, and it has helped me find hope in every negative situation.

"Every adversity, every failure, every heartache carries with it the seed of an equal or greater benefit."

We grow from adversity both in character and comfort zone. When things are going well, we enjoy the journey, but we are not growing. These times are important as we need to rest and recover. But it's in the tough times when we grow. We learn from mistakes, not when things are going well.

When you go through adversity, know that you are growing. Embrace this time and remind yourself that when you come through it, you will be stronger and wiser.

Thought for Today

Embrace the tough times and know that you are growing.

When you are not under pressure, you are resting and recovering – enjoy that time. Today think about the story of the bag of gold, which was the reward after the hard work of moving the stone. This is what you receive when you go through tough times if you look for it. Think about a negative situation – can you find the seed of something positive?

Today's Reflection

_____
_____
_____
_____
_____
_____
_____
_____
_____
_____

THE STARFISH

*O*nce upon a time, there was a man who used to go to the ocean to do his writing. He had a habit of walking on the beach before he began his work.

One day, as he was walking along the shore, he looked down the beach and saw a human figure moving like a dancer. He smiled to himself at the thought of someone who would dance to the day, and so, he walked faster to catch up.

As he got closer, he noticed that the figure was that of a young man and that what he was doing was not dancing at all. The young man was reaching down to the shore, picking up small objects, and throwing them into the ocean.

He came closer still and called out, 'Good morning! May I ask what it is that you are doing?' The young man paused, looked up, and replied, 'Throwing starfish into the ocean.'

'I must ask, then, why are you throwing starfish into the ocean?' asked the somewhat startled man. To this, the young man replied, 'The sun is up, and the tide is going out. If I don't throw them in, they'll die.'

Upon hearing this, the man commented, 'But, young man, do you not realize that there are miles and miles of beach and there are starfish all along every mile? You can't possibly make a difference!'

At this, the young man bent down, picked up yet another starfish, and threw it into the ocean. As it met the water, he said, 'It made a difference for that one.'

What a wonderful story to help us cope with the immense need in the world. We can't change the world, but we can change one life and then another and another, one at a time.

So, can I encourage you to take the time to do something that will make a difference to someone else's life ... and it doesn't have to be much, and they don't need to know. Just take a moment, do something special.

Thought for Today

Do you sometimes think that what you do won't make a difference?

There are so many needs in the world; it is easy to tell ourselves that we can't make a difference. But that attitude will result in nothing ever being done. Today think about people around you. Is there anyone you can bless with a kind word or a kind deed? It could be as small as commenting on how good they look or something practical. See if you can make a difference to one person today.

Today's Reflection

_____

THE FIVE-STAR CHEF

"*Narayanan Krishnan, all of 29 years old, does what he was professionally trained to do as a chef. Feed people. Only Krishnan does not do this in the swanky confines of a 5-star hotel.*

Every day, he wakes up at 4 am, cooks a simple hot meal, and then, along with his team, loads it in a van and travels about 200 km feeding the homeless in Madurai, Tamil Nadu.

Krishnan feeds, often with his hands, almost 400 destitute people every day. And for those who need it, he provides a free haircut too. He was selected as one of the Top 10 "CNN heroes 2010" list.

According to CNN, this award-winning chef with a five-star hotel chain was all set to go to Switzerland for a high-profile posting. On a visit to a Madurai temple, he came across a homeless, old man eating his own human waste. That stark sight changed Krishnan's life.

Much to the dismay of his parents, CNN says, Krishnan abandoned his career plans and decided to spend his life and his professional training in looking after those who could not care for themselves.

He has provided more than 1.2 million hot meals through his non-profit organisation Akshaya Trust, and now hopes to extend this to shelter for the homeless too."

Wow, this story blew me away because this man had it all and yet gave it all up to help others. I have often said that the 'true way to happiness is helping others.'

I believe if you can spend some of your time helping others and making a difference, then true happiness can be found. I have come across many stories of millionaires who have committed suicide. These were millionaires with more money than they could spend, but that wasn't enough!

Thought for Today

The way to true happiness is helping those in need.

Something unique happens when you help someone
in need. It may be something practical which takes
time and is a challenge. It could be spending time
with someone just listening to them. It could be
giving someone a lift. Whatever it is, try it and see
how it makes you feel.

Today's Reflection

_____

_____

_____

_____

_____

_____

_____

_____

_____

_____

_____

SUICIDE JUMPER SURVIVES

Since 1937, more than 2,000 people have lost their lives on the Golden Gate Bridge in San Francisco. Kevin Hines, miraculously, isn't one of them. Pushed to the brink by depression and anxiety, his mental illness finally got the best of him, and he decided he couldn't take it anymore.

He decided to commit suicide and jump from Golden Gate Bridge.

As he stood on the bridge, he watched people walking and driving past him. One woman stopped to talk to him but only to ask if he would take her picture.

Kevin explains, "I thought, growing up, that everything's going to be great. Then at 17, it all came crashing down." If you can imagine, feeling that everyone around you is out to get you, trying to hurt you, and trying to kill you. And you believe that to be the truth.

"From the extreme paranoia, I exhibited symptoms of mania. From the mania came hallucinations, both auditory and visual. And so with that and the bipolar disorder, I was just spiralling out of control."

"I vividly remember writing my suicide note. People don't get it. I thought I was a burden to everyone who loved me. Because that's what my brain told me. That's how powerful your brain is."

Kevin was desperate, but he didn't think anyone cared. "The reality is that everyone cared. I just couldn't see it."

"What I'm about to say," Kevin shared about his suicide attempt, "is the exact same thing that 19 Golden Gate Bridge survivors have also said. The millisecond my hands left the rail, there was instant regret. And I remember thinking. No one is going to know that I didn't want to die.

Kevin jumped, plummeting 25 stories down at 75mph, experiencing the worst pain in his life as he hit the water below, crushing his spinal vertebrae and breaking an ankle. But somehow, for some reason, Kevin survived. Even the first responders knew this was a miracle.

"The coast guard. . . said, 'Do you know how many people we pull out of this water who are already dead?' The guy put his hand on my forehead and said, 'Kid you're a miracle.'"
And now, Kevin shares his story in order to help others.

How he's using his second chance to bring awareness and understanding about mental illness is POWERFUL!

Thought for Today

A painful experience can lead to purpose and passion

What have you been through in your life which
has gone wrong? Whatever you have suffered gives
you empathy for those facing the same situation.
Think about those very painful times in your life and
see if you could use those to help others in similar
situations. Turn a negative into a positive because
you are uniquely positioned to help.

Today's Reflection

Oprah Winfrey:

"You become what you believe."

THE SHARK EXPERIMENT

During a research experiment, a marine biologist placed a shark into a large holding tank and then released several small bait fish into the tank. As you would expect, the shark quickly swam around the tank, attacked and ate the smaller fish.

The marine biologist then inserted a strong piece of clear fibreglass into the tank, creating two separate partitions. She then put the shark on one side of the fibreglass and a new set of bait fish on the other.

Again, the shark quickly attacked. This time, however, the shark slammed into the fibreglass divider and bounced off. Undeterred, the shark kept repeating this behaviour every few minutes to no avail. Meanwhile, the bait fish swam around unharmed in the second partition. Eventually, about an hour into the experiment, the shark gave up.

This experiment was repeated several dozen times over the next few weeks. Each time, the shark got less aggressive and made fewer attempts to attack the bait fish, until eventually, the shark got tired of hitting the fibreglass divider and simply stopped attacking altogether.

The marine biologist then removed the fiberglass divider, but the shark didn't attack. The shark was trained to believe a barrier existed between it and the bait fish, so the bait fish swam wherever they wished, free from harm.

Many of us, after experiencing setbacks and failures, emotionally give up and then stop trying altogether. Like the shark in the story, we believe that because we were unsuccessful in the past, we will always be unsuccessful. In other words, we continue to see a barrier, even when no 'real' barrier exists between where we are and where we want to go.

We can create a new belief system and a new future by changing the way we **Think**, the way we **Speak**, and the way we **Act**.

Thought for Today

You create your own belief system.

The experiences you've had throughout your life have created the belief system you have regarding what you can and can't achieve. Today think about some of the things you find difficult and see if there is a link to past negative experiences which you are anchored to. To create a new belief system, you need to think, speak, and act more positively.

Today's Reflection

_____

_____

_____

_____

_____

_____

_____

_____

_____

_____

_____

_____

THE WISE OLD MAN

"*The story is told of a wise old man. Every day he and his granddaughter would sit outside his petrol station in rocking chairs, waiting to greet tourists as they passed through their small town.*

One day a tall man with the appearance of a tourist started looking around like he was checking out the area for a place to live. 'So what kind of town is this anyway?' he asked. The old man replied, 'well, what kind of town are you from?' The man replied, 'One where the people are critical of each other. It's a real negative place to live.'

The old man said, 'You know, that's just how this town is too.' Later, a family passing through also stopped for petrol. The father stepped out and asked the old man, 'Is this town a good place to live?' The old man asked him about the town he currently lived in.

The man said, 'Where I'm from everyone's close, and always willing to lend a helping hand. I really hate to leave it.' The old man smiled and said, 'You know what, that's a lot like this town.'

After the family drove off, the old man's granddaughter asked, 'Grandpa, how come you told the first man that this was a terrible place to live, and when the second family asked, you told them it was a wonderful place to live?'

The old man looked into her big blue eyes and said, 'Sweetheart, no matter where you go, you take your attitude with you, and that's what makes it terrible or wonderful.'

Attitude or mindset is like an internal rudder of your life, which steers you down a negative or positive path. A positive mindset has high energy, and a negative mindset has low energy.

Are your thoughts, words, and actions more positive or more negative? You become what you think about all day long. Your thoughts and words determine where you head in life and also how you are perceived by others. If you want to change your life, change your words.

Thought for Today

You take your Attitude with you.

No matter where you go in life, you take yourself with you. You can't escape you. Your thoughts and your attitude follow you wherever you go. If your thoughts and words are negative, you spread those around you, and if they are positive, you spread those around you. Today think about this and observe what you are spreading around you.

Today's Reflection

_____
_____
_____
_____
_____
_____
_____
_____
_____
_____
_____
_____

BE THANKFUL

I came across these thoughts on thankfulness recently, and it really struck a chord with me.

"Be thankful that you don't already have everything you desire ... if you did, what would there be to look forward to?

Be thankful when you don't know something ... for it gives you the opportunity to learn.

Be thankful for the difficult times ... during those times you grow.

Be thankful for your limitations ... they give you opportunities for improvement.

Be thankful for each new challenge... which will build your strength and character.

Be thankful for your mistakes ... they will teach you valuable lessons.

Be thankful when you're tired and weary ... because it means you've given your all.

It's easy to be thankful for the 'good' things ... yet, a life of rich fulfilment comes to those who are thankful for the setbacks.

Gratitude can turn a negative into a positive ... find a way to be thankful for your troubles, and they can become your blessings."

I love the way Gratitude can change your state from negative to positive. Whenever you face something which is negative, just think about all the things you are grateful for, and you will soon start to feel more positive.

Your conscious mind is directly connected to your feelings, so when you think of something you are grateful for, you start to feel better. Conversely, when you think of anything which is negative, you feel worse.

The conscious mind can only think of one thing at a time. When you are focused on something stressful, you feel negative, but as you shift your focus to something positive, you have to stop thinking about that negative situation and switch to the positive thought or image, and by default, you start to feel better.

There is much evidence to demonstrate that people who are grateful are more optimistic and positive about their lives, are more physically active, and report fewer visits to a doctor.

Focusing on the positive and feeling grateful can improve your sleep quality and reduce feelings of anxiety and depression. Furthermore, levels of gratitude correlate to better moods and less fatigue and inflammation, reducing the risk of heart failure, even for those who are susceptible.

Thought for Today

What can you be thankful for today?

An attitude of Gratitude is very powerful and does change the way you feel. Today think about all the things in your life which you are grateful for. Who is in your life? What things do you own? What places do you love to visit? What food and drinks do you really enjoy? As you focus on these, observe how you start to feel better.

Today's Reflection

_____

_____

_____

_____

_____

_____

_____

_____

_____

_____

_____

_____

THE BAG OF MARBLES

"*Once upon a time, there was a foolish boy who had a bag full of beautiful marbles. Now, this boy was quite proud of his marbles. In fact, he thought so much of them that he would neither play with them himself, nor would he let anyone else play with them.*

He only took them out of the bag in order to count and admire them; they were never used for their intended purpose. Yet that boy carried that coveted bag of marbles everywhere he went.

Well, there was also a wise boy who wished he could have such a fine bag of marbles. So this boy worked hard and earned money to purchase a nice bag to hold marbles. Even though he had not yet earned enough with which to purchase any marbles, he had faith and purchased the marble bag.

He took special care of the bag and dreamed of the day it would contain marbles with which he could play and share with his friends.

Alas, the foolish boy with all of the marbles, didn't take care of the marble bag itself, and one day the bag developed a hole in the bottom seam. Still, he paid no attention, and, one by one, the marbles fell out of the bag.

It didn't take long, once the foolish boy's marble bag developed a hole, for the wise boy to begin to find those beautiful marbles, one at a time, lying unnoticed on the ground. And, one by one, he added them to his marble bag.

The wise boy thus gained a fine bag full of marbles in no time at all. This boy played with the marbles and shared them with all of his friends. And he always took special care of the bag, so he wouldn't lose any."

Because the foolish boy was selfish and careless, he lost all of his marbles and was left holding the bag. He spent so much time selfishly keeping the marbles to himself and not sharing them with others; he forgot to look after the bag. After all, the bag wasn't beautiful and shiny, so he thought it had no value, but little did he know how important that bag was.

Thought for Today

It is often the small insignificant things which are the most important.

We are often drawn to the bright shiny things in life, and we tend to ignore the boring functional things. If we ignore the basic things in life, we will slowly but surely fall apart. Things like good time management, good eating habits, good sleep habits. Watching how much we drink and how much we rest. Today think about what do you need to pay attention to?

Today's Reflection

_____
_____
_____
_____
_____
_____
_____
_____
_____
_____

TWO WORDS TO DESCRIBE YOU

It takes a disciplined spirit to endure the monastery on Montserrat in Spain. One of the fundamental requirements of this religious order is that the young men must maintain silence. Opportunities to speak are scheduled once every two years, at which time they are allowed to speak only two words.

One young initiate in this religious order, who had completed his first two years of training, was invited by his superior to make his first two-word presentation. "Food terrible," he said. Two years later, the invitation was once again extended.

The young man used this forum to exclaim, "Bed lumpy." Arriving at his superior's office two years later, he proclaimed, "I quit." The superior looked at this young monk and said, "You know, it doesn't surprise me a bit. All you've done since you arrived is complain, complain, complain."

Exaggerated? Maybe. What if you were asked to share two words that describe your life? Would your focus be the lumps, bumps, and unfairness, or are you committed to dwell on those things that are good, right, and lovely?

What we focus on is what we receive and eventually become. Focus on the positive, and life seems to work much better. This is a powerful message to internalise. 'What we See and what we Say is what we Get.' This is my quote and something I live by.

At the beginning of this book, I referenced some research findings on the benefits of positive thinking, and the evidence is clear to demonstrate that we live a happier, healthier, and more balanced life if we focus on the positive rather than on the negative.

Remember, what we think about affects our feelings. If we focus on something positive, we feel better, if we focus on something negative, we feel worse. A phrase often repeated is, **'you become what you think about all day long."** - Ralph Waldo Emerson

Thought for Today

Do you focus more on the positives in life or more on the negatives?

What two words would you use to describe yourself? Think about this today and see what you come up with. Go deep with this and see if you can think of a couple of words which honestly describe you. When you look at these two words, are you happy with them? If not, find two new words, then start working to become them.

Today's Reflection

YOU HAVE AMAZING POTENTIAL

A mother and a baby camel were lying around under a tree. Then the baby camel asked, "Why do camels have humps?"

The mother camel considered this and said, "We are desert animals, so we have the humps to store water so that we can survive with very little water." The baby camel thought for a moment then said, "Ok...why, are our legs long and our feet rounded?"

The mama replied, "They are meant for walking in the desert." The baby paused. After a beat, the baby camel asked, "Why are our eyelashes long? Sometimes they get in my way." The mama responded, "Those long thick eyelashes protect your eyes from the desert sand when it blows in the wind."

The baby thought and thought. Then he said, "I see. So, the hump is to store water when we are in the desert, the legs are for walking through the desert, and these eyelashes protect my eyes from the desert - then why do we live in the Zoo?"

It's an amusing story but one which has a lesson.

The Lesson: *Skills and abilities are only useful if you are in the right place at the right time. Otherwise, they go to waste.*

What skills and abilities do you have? Are they being used where you are right now? If not, is there something you can do to utilise your gifts? Can you bring this to the attention of who you work for? Can you start a business from home? Can you change your job and find one which really suits your skillset? Can you volunteer for some amazing charity?

These are big questions, but life is short and Mental Resilience is about taking life by the scruff of the neck and giving it all you have. It is not for everyone, but sometimes it's good to take stock of your life and check that you are happy with the path you are travelling. If not, then there is no harm in spending some time looking at options which could create a real passion and joy to your life.

I am not advocating that you do anything reckless but suggest that you examine your life and double-check that you are happy with the road you are travelling.

Thought for Today

Do you believe you have reached the very peak of your potential for your life?

Do you think there is more you can yet achieve? If so, what is it? Today think about your life and your potential. Is there more you can do before it's too late? We are all going to die one day, and there will come a time when we can't do much. Take time now while you have your health and energy to fulfil some of your dreams. What are they?

Today's Reflection

_____

_____

_____

_____

_____

_____

_____

_____

_____

_____

FROM JANITOR TO PRINCIPAL

In November 2013, Gabe Sonnier was made the principal at Port Barre Elementary School in Port Barre, LA.

Sonnier's 30-year ride from janitor to principal began in 1985 when the principal at the time, Westley Jones, told Sonnier he should be "grading papers [rather than] picking them up."

Sonnier said no one had believed so strongly in him before, so he took Westley's words as inspiration. At 39 years-old, Sonnier began spending all of his free time studying.

"I would come to work at like 5 in the morning and leave at 7 [am] and go to school all day and then come back and finish up my eight hours of work here, and then go home and do homework," Sonnier told TV station KATC.

Sonnier eventually got his teaching degree, his first job as a teacher, his Master's Degree, and now he's the principal.

Sonnier advises others to think bigger: he credits Westley Jones' support and mentorship with inspiring him to get his dream job. Encouragement is a powerful force. A force that Sonnier and his students are thankful for.

What a great story of inspiration and how working hard and believing in yourself can create an amazing life. Your life is run by your belief system, and you can only go as far as you believe you can. To achieve more in your life, you need first to believe you can; then you take the action to make it happen.

Your belief system is like a rudder of your life and it steers you in the direction of your beliefs about yourself. To change the way your life is heading you need to change your belief (rudder) and this will then change the course of your life. I was decorating to pay the bills then I changed my belief about what I could achieve and became an author and international speaker.

Someone told me that I had what it takes to make a success of my business. These words were spoken to me while I was still decorating to make ends meet. These words lit a fire in my belly, and that flame wouldn't go out. I fanned that flame, and slowly but surely, my life started to turn around. I had to believe that I could succeed long before I saw it in reality.

Thought for Today

Encouraging words have the power to change lives.

Today think about the times you have been encouraged in the past and what this meant to you. Try to remember specific people who spoke these words. Encouragement can make a huge difference in people's lives, and I want you to think who you could encourage today. Make it your mission to encourage someone, and as you do, you will experience the wonderful feelings from this simple act.

Today's Reflection

_____

_____

_____

_____

_____

_____

_____

_____

_____

_____

_____

THINGS AREN'T ALWAYS WHAT THEY SEEM

"*Two travelling angels stopped to spend the night in the home of a wealthy family.*

The family was rude and refused to let the angels stay in the mansion's guest room. Instead, the angels were given a small space in the cold basement. As they made their bed on the hard floor, the older angel saw a hole in the wall and repaired it. When the younger angel asked why, the older angel replied,

"Things aren't always what they seem."

The next night, the angels came to rest at the house of a very poor, but very hospitable farmer and his wife. After sharing what little food they had, the couple let the angels sleep in their bed so they could have a good night's rest.

When the sun came up the next morning, the angels found the farmer and his wife in tears. Their only cow, whose milk had been their sole income, lay dead in the field.

The younger angel was infuriated and asked the older angel how she could have let this happen. "The first man had everything, yet you helped him," he accused. "The second family had little but was willing to share everything, and you let the cow die."

226

"Things aren't always what they seem," the older angel replied.

"When we stayed in the basement of the mansion, I noticed there was gold stored in that hole in the wall. Since the owner was so obsessed with greed and unwilling to share his good fortune, I sealed the wall so he wouldn't find it.

"Then last night as we slept in the farmer's bed, the angel of death came for his wife. I gave him the cow instead.

"Things aren't always what they seem."

When things don't turn out exactly the way you think they should, have faith. Trust that every outcome is always to your advantage. You just might not know it until sometime later, as this inspiring story eloquently attests."

It may not make sense at the time, but if you are patient, have faith, and look for that seed, you will find it. When you find that seed of something positive, it will give you hope and the energy to keep going.

Thought for Today

Today try to find a positive in any negative situation you face.

There is always a seed of something positive in every negative situation. Today focus on trying to find something positive in an adversity you face. See if you can take a moment to pause and look for that 'At Least Moment' where at least something good came out of the situation.

Today's Reflection

_____

_____

_____

_____

_____

_____

_____

_____

_____

_____

_____

_____

_____

MAGIC JOHNSON

I had a dream to meet the best basketball player in the world in the mid 1980s, but I didn't know how this could be achieved. At the time, I had just joined a local radio station in Newcastle called Metro FM and was working in the sales department.

This dream of meeting this legend wouldn't go away, and eventually, I decided to call the Los Angeles Lakers and see if I could get them to agree for me to interview Magic. I called and was put through to the PR Manager, and I explained who I was and what I wanted to do.

Luckily for me, he misunderstood and thought that I worked for the BBC in London and immediately offered me an **'Access All Areas'** pass for a week! This was amazing and meant I could spend the entire week with the team attending practice sessions, watching the games free of charge, and interviewing the players after the games.

I had the opportunity to meet the great players of that time, and I still have the photograph of Magic Johnson and me together after one of the matches. To watch the greatest player in history up to that time live was simply amazing, and to also spend time with him and the team was a once in a lifetime experience.

It was probably the most spectacular week up to this point in my life. It took some courage to call the Los Angeles Lakers and to stay calm during the conversation, but because I did, I ended up achieving far more than I could have ever dreamed. To watch and personally hang out with the greatest player in the world was something I will never forget.

When you have Mental Resilience and a strong self-belief, you take on more challenges than the average person. When you do this by the law of averages, more opportunities present themselves. If I hadn't had a vision to meet Magic Johnson (which was a powerful driver) and the confidence to pick up the phone, some 'Magic' moments would have passed me by, and I would have missed some of the most exciting days of my life.

Thought for Today

What do you really want in life?

Do you have the confidence to go for the things you desire? Today think about any dreams you have. Maybe someone you want to meet or something you really want to do or an amazing country you want to visit. I have a long list of things I am working through, and it is exciting to be achieving many new and incredible things.

Today's Reflection

_____

_____

_____

_____

_____

_____

_____

_____

_____

_____

_____

_____

THE 4 SEASONS OF LIFE

"*There was a man who had four sons. He wanted his sons to learn not to judge things too quickly. So he sent them each on a quest, in turn, to go and look at a pear tree that was a great distance away.*

The first son went in the winter, the second in the spring, the third in summer, and the youngest son in the autumn.

When they had all gone and come back, he called them together to describe what they had seen.

The first son said that the tree was ugly, bent, and twisted.

The second son said no – it was covered with green buds and full of promise.

The third son disagreed; he said it was laden with blossoms that smelled so sweet and looked so beautiful, it was the most graceful thing he had ever seen.

The last son disagreed with all of them; he said it was ripe and drooping with fruit, full of life and fulfilment.

The man then explained to his sons that they were all right because they had each seen but one season in the tree's life. He told them that you cannot judge a tree, or a person, by only one season, and that the essence of who they are – and the pleasure, joy, and love that come from that life – can only be measured at the end when all the seasons are up.

If you give up when it's winter, you will miss the promise of your spring, the beauty of your summer, fulfilment of your autumn.

Don't judge a life by one difficult season. Don't let the pain of one season destroy the joy of all the rest."

In life, we will experience many positive things and many negative things. I believe that we learn much more from negative experiences than we do from positive ones. We enjoy the positive times and learn from the negative times.

The only time we grow in character and comfort zone is when we are under pressure. Don't be held back by your belief system, which may be telling you that you can't do it, or you will fail. This belief system is created during your lifetime and is like a rudder steering a ship. Your belief system determines how far you go in life.

Thought for Today

How do you view tough winter times in your life?

Embrace the tough times knowing that you are growing through the process. How you perceive things is how you experience them. Seasons pass, and each one brings in the next. In life, we experience highs and lows, but they don't last. It is part of life's journey that we go through various seasons in our life, yet each one has its own beauty.

Today's Reflection

_____

_____

_____

_____

_____

_____

_____

_____

_____

_____

_____

_____

Willie Nelson:

"Once you replace negative thoughts with positive ones, you'll start having positive results."

10-YEAR-OLD CREATES
HER OWN DREAM BOARD!

A year after one of my Masterclasses, I met up with one of the attendees, and he recounted the time he spent with his family after my Mental Resilience Masterclass.

He told me that when he got home following this session, he sat his family down and discussed everything I had shared.

The information he shared really inspired them and his 10-year-old daughter decided there and then to create her own Dream Board and look at it every day to see if she could achieve some things on it. She found pictures to represent her dreams and put them on the board.

"My dad came home from work one day and gave me a Basketball signed by John Dabrowski, and he explained how he had got it. When I first got the basketball, I was delighted, and so later that day I made my Dream Board, this included improving my Maths, being Head Girl at my school, going to Cambridge University and become a Doctor.

I asked my mum to buy me a glass frame so that I could put the picture of my Dream Board into it and look at it every night. I also put the basketball that my dad won during John's event, next to the Glass frame, and looked at that as well.

One of my dreams was to be Head Girl at my school, so to achieve that dream, I asked the current Head Girl what she had to do to become Head Girl, and this helped me make up my mind. My dreams became a reality when I was told by the Headmaster on Speech day that I was chosen as Head Girl.

I also have improved my maths by 20% over the year, so it just shows you my motto works. 'If you believe, you will achieve,' and from that day forward, there is nothing I cannot do."

Wow, how unbelievable is that? I know from my personal experience that your mind is extremely powerful, and you can achieve amazing things if you truly believe you can.

At just ten years of age, this girl is now on an exciting path because she understands the importance of having a positive mindset and the power of the Dream Board. I can't wait to see what she achieves next.

Thought for Today

What do you want to achieve in the next 20 years?

If you have a Dream Board, then think about another picture to add to it. If you don't, why not start one today? When you have a Dream Board, and you visualise yourself having achieved these dreams, you engage your Reticular Activating System, which brings the things you visualise into your conscious mind. This increases the chance of success. Feel free to email me for more information on this at john@jdmindcoach.com

Today's Reflection

_____

_____

_____

_____

_____

_____

_____

_____

_____

INTEGRITY FOR LIFE

I came across this story of another doing the right thing. Bobby Jones could have cheated to win the US Open, but he had great integrity and refused to live that way.

Bobby Jones is considered one of history's greatest golfers. But more than all his victories on the golf course, he's famous for what happened in the 1925 U.S Open. He inadvertently touched his ball and assessed himself a one-stroke penalty, even though no one else saw him touch the ball.

But he couldn't violate his conscience. And by assessing himself that penalty, he lost the Open by just one stroke. When tournament officials tried to compliment him for his integrity, Jones simply said, 'You might as well praise me for not breaking into banks. There is only one way to play this game.'

Bobby Jones played by the rules. Full Stop. And in doing so, he honoured the integrity of the game. One sportswriter wrote, 'In the opinion of many people, of all the great athletes, Bobby Jones came the closest to what we call a great man.'

Jones could have won the tournament, but he would have lost his integrity. And winning the U.S Open wasn't worth a one-stroke penalty on his integrity. That's epic integrity! And that's something to be celebrated.

We live in a culture that celebrates talent more than integrity, but we've got it backwards. Talent depreciates over time, so do intellect and appearance. You will eventually lose your strength and looks. You may even lose your mind.

But you don't have to lose your integrity. Integrity is the only thing that doesn't depreciate over time. Nothing takes longer to build than a good reputation. And nothing is destroyed more quickly by lack of integrity.

That's why your integrity must be celebrated and protected above all else.

You may succeed financially, but if you compromise your integrity, you will experience a feeling of uneasiness, and there will be a lack of joy and peace in your life. You will be able to hide this most of the time, but in those times when you reflect, you will remember those occasions where you have compromised, and it can really affect your peace and happiness.

Thought for Today

Integrity is the bedrock of a happy, fulfilled life.

What you sow is what you reap - so sow well. Today
think about all the little decisions you make daily
and check your integrity on each one. The little
white lie is still a little white lie. This can be a touchy
subject, and most people don't see why they need
integrity. What I know is: when you do the right
thing, good things happen. What do you think?

Today's Reflection

_____

_____

_____

_____

_____

_____

_____

_____

_____

_____

_____

HOW TO OVERCOME FEAR

"Yesterday AND tomorrow both clamour for our attention. Yesterday wants us to second-guess our decisions and worry if we did the right thing. That's wasted energy. As President Harry Truman said, 'If you've done the best you can – if you've done what you have to do – there's no use worrying about it because nothing can change it.'

And tomorrow can also cause you to miss opportunities. Let's face it; most people arrive at a different destination in life than what they expected – some better, some worse, but all different. So, focussing on the destination isn't necessarily a good idea. Besides, tomorrow may come, or it may not. There are no guarantees.

The only place you really have any power – is in the present. Do what you can in the here and now despite your fear, and you'll have the satisfaction of knowing you're doing everything within your power to reach your potential.

If you project too far into the future, you'll suffer from the 'what ifs?' and your fear runs wild. American author Mark Twain quipped, 'I've been through some horrible things in my life – a few of which actually happened!'

Every day fear and faith will rise inside you, and you get to decide which one will prevail. Somebody wrote, 'Two natures beat within my breast; one is foul the other is blessed. The one I love, the other I hate; the one I feed will dominate.'

Fear and faith will always be present in your life, and the one you feed will come out on top. You can't expect fear to simply disappear. If you focus on your fears, entertain them, give in to them, they'll increase.

The way to overcome them is to starve them. Don't give them your time or energy. Don't feed them with gossip, negative news reports, or frightening films. Focus on your faith and feed your mind with positive thoughts and images."

Thought for Today

Thinking about yesterday or tomorrow increases stress.

The only power you have is today, so use it to change your tomorrow. Stress occurs when we are either thinking back or thinking forwards. We can't change the past, and the future hasn't arrived yet, so the only real power you have is Now. Today be aware of how much time you spend thinking about past events or worrying about the future. What you do today directly affects your future.

Today's Reflection

_____

_____

_____

_____

_____

_____

_____

_____

_____

_____

A DOG'S PURPOSE

*B*eing *a veterinarian, I had been called to examine a
ten-year-old Irish Wolfhound named Belker. The dog's
owners, Ron, his wife Lisa, and their little boy Shane, were all
very attached to Belker, and they were hoping for a miracle.*

*I examined Belker and found he was dying of cancer. I told
the family we couldn't do anything for Belker and offered to
perform the euthanasia procedure for the old dog in their
home.*

*As we made arrangements, Ron and Lisa told me they
thought it would be good for six-year-old Shane to observe
the procedure. They felt as though Shane might learn
something from the experience.*

*The next day, I felt the familiar catch in my throat as Belker's
family surrounded him. Shane seemed so calm, petting the
old dog for the last time, that I wondered if he understood
what was going on. Within a few minutes, Belker slipped
peacefully away.*

*The little boy seemed to accept Belker's transition without
any difficulty or confusion. We sat together for a while after
Belker's death, wondering aloud about the sad fact that
animal lives are shorter than human lives. Shane, who had
been listening quietly, piped up, 'I know why.'*

Startled, we all turned to him. What came out of his mouth next stunned me. I'd never heard a more comforting explanation.

He said, 'People are born so that they can learn how to live a good life -- like loving everybody all the time and being nice, right?' The six-year-old continued, 'Well, dogs already know how to do that, so they don't have to stay as long.'

Live simply.
Love generously.
Care deeply.
Speak kindly.

This is all much easier said than done - but we can all take something from this and apply it to our lives, and if we do, we will live much happier, more fulfilled lives. Life is to be enjoyed and to make a difference.

Thought for Today

Live simply, Love generously, Care deeply, Speak kindly.

A simple act of kindness can make a huge difference to someone's life. Today as you go about your day, observe any kindness from other people. If you notice something, notice how it makes you feel. Also, do something nice for someone. A simple loving life can be the most amazing way to live. There is something special about being content in life.

Today's Reflection

_____

_____

_____

_____

_____

_____

_____

_____

_____

_____

IF A DOG WERE THE TEACHER, YOU WOULD LEARN THINGS LIKE:

*When loved ones come home, always run to greet them.
Never pass up the opportunity to go for a joyride.
Allow the experience of fresh air and the wind in your face to be pure Ecstasy.
Take naps.
Stretch before rising.
Run, romp, and play daily.
Thrive on attention and let people touch you.
Avoid biting when a simple growl will do.
On warm days, stop to lie on your back on the grass.
On hot days, drink lots of water and lie under a shady tree.
When you're happy, dance around and wag your entire body...
Delight in the simple joy of a long walk.
Be loyal.
Never pretend to be something you're not.
If what you want lies buried, dig until you find it.
When someone is having a bad day, be silent, sit close by, and nuzzle them gently.*

What a great description of a loyal happy dog. We can learn a lot from this as you don't find many stressed dogs. We need to rest more and play more and simply enjoy being.

Mental Resilience is much more than just coping with stress; it's very much about stopping the stress building in the first place. We need to look at ways where we can relax and be at peace.

Mindfulness is a wonderful thing and is all about being in the moment, non-judgmentally, observing things around us. In this state, we cannot be stressed. The conscious mind can only think of one thing at a time so when you are focussed on something nearby you cannot be thinking about your stressful situations.

If you can be mindful many times a day you create moments of peace and stillness which help you maintain a good balance between work and rest. Your mind needs to take regular breaks as does your body. Exercise is good for the body and mindfulness is good for the mind.

Thought for Today

See how many times you can stop and simply observe something around you.

Take a look at the list above and see if you can apply some of these in your life. When you are mindful, you cannot be stressed as the conscious mind can only think of one thing at a time. As we lose ourselves in the beauty of nature or something else of interest, we let go of everything and experience a few moments of perfect peace.

Today's Reflection

_____
_____
_____
_____
_____
_____
_____
_____
_____
_____
_____

THE IMPORTANCE OF A POSITIVE INNER VOICE

I have already mentioned that one thing I do at the start of each day is to take time to read something motivational. It gets me in a good place, and I know that if I spend this quiet time first thing no matter how big my priority list is, then I have a good and productive day.

My wedding day was no exception and was perfect in every way imaginable. The service at Kilburn Hall was magnificent, the guests were incredibly special people to us, and all were very carefully selected as we could only invite 48 guests. There were so many more people important to us we wanted to invite but just couldn't.

On the morning of the wedding, I wrote my speech and then wrote my blog and finally arrived 20 minutes before the ceremony was due to start. It was cutting it a bit fine, but I had visualised everything going well on the day, so I was calm and relaxed.

Julie looked stunning as she came down the stairs, and we enjoyed every moment of the day. I had written my speech in an hour in the morning, and before I knew it, I was on my feet delivering the speech. I had no time to practice or even read through it, but I trusted myself that I would find the right words that they would come to me, and they did. For me, it proved the importance of a positive inner voice.

Finding and marrying the right partner was on my Dream Board, and the wedding picture is one more I can tick off. I've had my fair share of ups and downs, and I truly believe that –

"It's not how you start in life that counts, but how you finish."

We all have an inner voice which never stops. We refer to it as thinking, and most of the words we speak to ourselves are negative by default. The vast majority of news items are negative as this type of news sells. We are bombarded with pessimistic messages continually. As we think about these stories, we start to create a negative inner voice pattern.

To counteract this, we can create a more positive inner voice using a series of positive statements repeated over and over during pressure situations. These help us perform better under extreme duress.

Thought for Today

Your inner voice can affect your performance

Today I want you to focus on your inner voice and think of a time when thinking positively has worked for you. I used to be extremely nervous in pressure situations, and it was during those times my inner voice was negative. When we experience situations where we are confident, our inner voice is naturally positive. So, to perform well under pressure, we need a positive inner voice.

Today's Reflection

_____

_____

_____

_____

_____

_____

_____

_____

_____

_____

_____

PREPARATION FOR YOUR FUTURE

"*W*hat you are doing right now might seem insignificant and unrewarding, but it could be preparing you for something in the future.*

When Daniel Webster started out as a lawyer, he took a case for a fee of just twenty dollars. The case turned out to be a very difficult one, and in preparing for it, he had to make a trip to Boston, which cost him more than twenty dollars. But he determined to do a thorough job and win the case, which he did.

Years later, a company approached him on short notice, asking him to undertake a case for which they were willing to pay him the largest fee he had ever received. In reviewing the case, he found it was almost identical to the one he'd researched and won nearly twenty years earlier, and for which he was paid only twenty dollars.

A great reward for seeing it through

He took the case, and just as before, the verdict was in favour of his client. When you do only what you feel like doing or enjoy doing, you can overlook relationships and undervalue experiences essential to your future.

Your destiny is made up of seemingly insignificant moments, experiences, and encounters. Your today is connected to your tomorrow, so maximise each opportunity and relationship that comes your way.

What a great phrase 'Your today is connected to your tomorrow.' Take a moment to let that sink in as it is profound. What you do today directly affects your future. If you are lazy and only do the bare minimum to get by, you will experience a very different future to the one you will experience if you work hard and smart and help other people along the way. It's not just about you; it's about those around you too.

If you want a happy, healthy future, you need to take the right actions to achieve that. Without sowing the right seeds, you won't reap a good harvest. Just because it seems insignificant, doesn't mean it is. The next insignificant task you take on could propel you to the next level.

Thought for Today

Don't miss amazing opportunities disguised as insignificant.

Pause to think and just check whether something may be significant. Your today is connected to your tomorrow, so maximise each opportunity and relationship that comes your way. You never know where things may lead, so think carefully before you say no to something and just check your gut to see if this could be a seed for the future.

Today's Reflection

_____

_____

_____

_____

_____

_____

_____

_____

_____

_____

_____

A GOOD ATTITUDE OPENS THE DOOR

*W*hen *Stanford researchers recently peered into the brains of students to see how attitude affects achievement, they found something startling. Your outlook on learning, it turns out, matters just as much as your IQ.*

Scientists and educators have long noted that kids who have a positive attitude towards maths do better in the subject, but is that just because easily passing tests naturally makes you enjoy something, or does the arrow of causation point the other way?

Does starting off with the expectation that you'll enjoy and be good at maths help you master numbers?

To start to tease this out, a research team out of Stanford recently analysed the math skills and attitudes of 240 kids aged seven to ten, as well as running 47 of them through an fMRI (Functional magnetic resonance imaging)machine while asking them to do some basic arithmetic. What did they find?

As expected, kids who did well in math liked math more, both according to self-reports and their parents, and kids who hated the subject did poorly. But the brain scans also turned up something much more fascinating.

The images revealed that the hippocampus, a brain area linked with memory and learning, was significantly more active in kids with a positive attitude towards math.

It appears it's not just that children like subjects they're good at. It's also that liking a subject helps students' brains work better.

"We think the relationship between positive attitude and math achievement is mutual, bi-directional," said Lang Chen, the study's lead author. "It's like bootstrapping: A good attitude opens the door to high achievement, which means you then have a better attitude, getting you into a good circle of learning."

But whatever the exact weight of various factors turns out to be, it's already clear that attitude has a bigger impact on performance than the scientists expected.

"Attitude is really important," said Chen, "Based on our data, the unique contribution of positive attitude to math achievement is as large as the contribution from IQ."

This very good current research again demonstrates the importance of a positive attitude. There is more and more evidence appearing to back this up, and even though 'Positive Thinking' has been around for hundreds of years, it's still one of the keys to success and happiness.

Thought for Today

A good attitude opens the door to high achievement.

When you are positive, you have more energy. When you have a higher level of energy, you achieve more. When you achieve more, you are more positive, so you have more energy, and the cycle continues. Today observe how you feel when you are positive and also when you are negative. See if you notice a change in your energy levels.

Today's Reflection

_____

_____

_____

_____

_____

_____

_____

_____

_____

_____

_____

_____

THE DOGSLED DERBY

I came across this article in Word for Today, and it struck a chord regarding the importance of focus. I am in the process of developing a second Mental Resilience masterclass, which builds on the first. One of the five key pillars of Mental Resilience described in the current masterclass is Focus.

In a small Wisconsin town on the southern shore of Lake Superior, the annual dogsled derby was about to begin. The racers were all children – from older boys with several dogs and big sleds to one little boy who had only a small sled and a dog.

On the signal, the sleds took off, and the little fellow was soon so far behind that he hardly seemed to be in the race at all. Then about halfway through the race when the second-place team tried to move into first place, the sleds got too close, and the dogs began to fight.

As each of the other sleds in the race came upon the fight, more dogs got involved. The scene was soon one big seething knot of kids, sleds, and dogs. All thought of racing had vanished from the minds of the racers.

However, the one little guy and his dog managed to skirt the others and went on to win the race.

RightPath® founder and business coach Jerry Mabe tells employers that when they hire managers, they should look out for 'shiny object' people. Why? Because like children, they are easily distracted by other things, and the job suffers under their watch.

To succeed you must stay focused on what's important and pursue your goals without wavering or hesitating. Keep your eyes on the finish line.

Laser-like focus is one of the 5 key pillars of Mental Resilience and is instrumental in the pursuit of goals and dreams. Whatever your dreams are - losing focus will deflect your attention and very soon you will find that the dream is fading, and it will eventually fade into the background.

As I write this book, I know without a shadow of a doubt that I require laser-like focus each day to achieve the writing targets I have set myself. I know from experience that a project can stretch to the urgency and focus you give to it. If you are relaxed and carefree a project, which should take two weeks, can take two months.

Thought for Today

Do you start something then lose interest?

Today think about your focus and how good you are at staying on target for long periods of time. Do you start well then let other things divert your attention from what you were focused on? Laser-like focus is a great attribute to success, and if you can develop this over time, you will be more successful as you move forward in life.

Today's Reflection

_____

_____

_____

_____

_____

_____

_____

_____

_____

_____

_____

_____

DON'T CHASE HAPPINESS

"*An old man lived in the village. He was one of the most unfortunate people in the world. The whole village was tired of him; he was always gloomy; he constantly complained and was permanently in a bad mood.*

The longer he lived, the viler he was becoming, and the more poisonous were his words. People avoided him because his misfortune became contagious. It was even unnatural and insulting to be happy next to him.

He created the feeling of unhappiness in others.

But one day, when he turned eighty years old, an incredible thing happened. Instantly everyone started hearing the rumour:

"The Old Man is happy today, he doesn't complain about anything, smiles, and even his face has freshened up."

The whole village gathered together. A villager asked the old man, 'What happened to you?'

"Nothing special. Eighty years I've been chasing happiness, and it was useless. And then I decided to live without happiness and just enjoy life. That's why I'm happy now."
Moral of the story: *Don't chase happiness. Enjoy your life."*

We can chase happiness all we want, but if we don't enjoy parts of each day, then we will always be waiting for the day when we will be happy. We need to capture moments in each day when we observe something beautiful like an autumn leaf or a beautiful sunset.

It may be eating or drinking something, or just kicking back on the sofa and watching TV. It may be going for a walk by yourself or with a loved one or eating dinner with loved ones. Happiness comes in small everyday things. We can take moments each day to be grateful for these amazing moments, and as we do this, we trigger the chemicals Dopamine and Serotonin, which makes us feel good.

Thought for Today

Are you too busy to capture the magic moments?

Life is passing you by, and each sunset is a day less
to live. We only have a set time to live our lives, and
no one knows when their time is up. Today try to
imagine this is your last day and see what you would
do if this were the case. Would you capture more
magic moments? Would you tell the people closest
to you that you love them? Would you spend more
time with people?

Today's Reflection

_____

_____

_____

_____

_____

_____

_____

_____

_____

_____

Richard Branson:

"Positive people don't just have a good day; they make it a good day. People who think positively usually see endless possibilities."

HOW THOUGHTS CAN CHANGE YOUR LIFE

I came across this article by Brian Tracey, the Canadian-American motivational public speaker, and self-development author. I agree with every word of this article:

"Let me ask you a question.

Can you guess what the most successful and happy people think about all day long?

The answer is quite simple... Healthy, happy people think about what they want and how to get it, most of the time. In this way, developing a positive attitude can truly change your entire life.

When you think and talk about what you want and how to get it, you feel happier and in greater control of your life. When you think about something that makes you happy, your brain actually releases endorphins, which give you a generalized feeling of well-being.
As a result, you develop a positive attitude.

Based on many psychological tests, happy people seem to have a special quality that enables them to live a better life than the average.

Can you guess what it is?

It's the quality of optimism!

The best news about optimism is that it is a learnable quality. That means you can learn how to think positive by adopting an optimistic mindset.

Optimists seem to have different ways of dealing with the world that set them apart from the average.

First, they keep their minds on what they want and keep looking for ways to get it.

Second, optimists look for the good in every problem or difficulty.

What we know is that, if you are looking for something good or beneficial in a person or situation, you will always find it. And while you are looking, you will be a more positive and cheerful person.

Optimists seek the valuable lesson in every setback or reversal. Rather than getting upset and blaming someone else for what has happened, they take control over their emotions by saying, "What can I learn from this experience?"

Resolve today to learn how to develop positive thinking and a positive attitude toward yourself, the people around you, and your life."

Thought for Today

Optimism is a learnable quality, so think about how you can develop it.

Today think about your level of optimism. Are you generally optimistic, or are you more pessimistic? Worldwide evidence shows that optimistic people are happier and healthier. Optimists keep their minds on what they want and keep looking for ways to get it. They also look for the good in every problem or difficulty.

Today's Reflection

_____

_____

_____

_____

_____

_____

_____

_____

_____

_____

_____

DAY 82

AN AMAZING STORY OF SELF-BELIEF

Bill Porter was an Oregon door-to-door salesman who plied his trade for decades despite having severe cerebral palsy. His story inspired an Emmy-winning television film 'Door to Door' starring William H. Macy.

"Bill was born in San Francisco on Sept. 9, 1932, to Ernest and Irene Porter; a birth injury left him with cerebral palsy. When he was a youth, the family settled in Portland, where Ernest Porter sold signs to local businesses.

After graduating from high school, Bill Porter, seeking work, was deemed unemployable by the state. The state offered him disability benefits. Mr. Porter declined.

Encouraged by his mother to pursue a sales career, he applied to the Fuller Brush Company but was turned away. The Watkins company turned him away, too, until Mr. Porter, in his first successful pitch, persuaded them to give him their most inhospitable territory in Portland.

He covered it by foot, taking the bus as close as he could get before disembarking to walk his route — eight to 10 miles daily. He had the use of only one hand; in it, he carried a briefcase filled with pictures of his products. A traditional sample case would have been too heavy.

Working on commission, he braved all weather and a spate of slammed doors. Little by little, the orders came, for soap and spices and dog biscuits. When the products arrived, his mother delivered them by car; in later years, when she could no longer manage the task, Mr. Porter hired Ms. Brady.

Ms. Brady, who had worked for Mr. Porter since 1980, witnessed a sterling example of his sales prowess in the late 1990s. They were trying to fly to a speaking engagement in Canada: lacking a photo ID, Mr. Porter was barred from boarding.

Anxious to make the next flight, they drove to Mr. Porter's home, unearthed his baptismal certificate, and raced to the Department of Motor Vehicles. A helpful clerk, who recognized Mr. Porter from local news coverage, fast-tracked his application for a non-driver ID.

In a matter of minutes, Ms. Brady recalled that Mr. Porter not only obtained his ID card but also sold the clerk a large tin of cinnamon."

What an amazing story of self-belief, commitment, discipline, hard work, and motivation. It demonstrates so well that 'it's not what happens to you that counts but how you choose to respond.'

Thought for Today

What difficulties are you currently facing?

Today think about Bill Porter and see if you can find some motivation from this amazing story. Does this put into perspective some of the things you are finding to be exceedingly difficult? Think about the kind of mindset Bill Porter had and what kind of work ethic he demonstrated. See if you can find the inspiration to try something you have given up on.

Today's Reflection

_____
_____
_____
_____
_____
_____
_____
_____
_____
_____
_____
_____

YOU CAN GROW OLD GRACEFULLY!

Four years ago I attended the funeral of the husband of one of my cousins. I drove to Wales with my mother, Janina, and my sister Chris. We had a pleasant journey, and as I watched my mother, I was amazed by how spritely she was at 93 years of age.

She is an excellent example of how you can grow old with grace and with a passion for life. She gets herself up in the morning and puts herself to bed at night. She washes herself and makes her own tea even now at the age of 97! I have pondered why she is doing so well and how she remains so cheerful. I have concluded that it must be her positive outlook and her genuine care for other people.

Whenever I go to see her, she is cheerful, and I have never heard her speak badly of anyone. I have noticed that if she doesn't have anything good to say, she won't say anything. Gossip is often the easiest way to make conversation, but it is not edifying or positive. It can be poisonous, and it damages the people who listen, the person who is gossiping, and the person being talked about indirectly.

I am in my sixties, and I aim to grow old gracefully and with a passion for life. I want to do as much as I can for as many people as I can before I depart. *What you see and What you say is What you get.* This is one of my favourite quotes, which I always write in my books when I sign them. It means that what you see in your mind and what you say determines how your life will work out.

Six years ago, I dramatically changed the way I think, speak, and act, and since then, my entire life has changed for the better. Good things seem to happen on a regular basis as opposed to bad things happening frequently. There is no scientific proof that this should work, but there are multiple thousands of happy people across the world who would testify how this process has changed their lives.

Thought for Today

What you see and what you say is what you get.

Today observe how you think and how you speak. Are you more positive or negative on average? If you are more positive, then today's principle will work for you. If you are more negative than positive, then it is likely that you may experience more negatives in your life.

Change the way you think and speak, and see what happens.

Today's Reflection

_____

_____

_____

_____

_____

_____

_____

_____

_____

_____

_____

FRANKLIN D. ROOSEVELT

When Franklin D. Roosevelt woke up on August 10, 1921, with plans to take his wife and three older children out for a sail in New Brunswick, Canada, he had no idea that it would be the last day he would have full use of his legs.

Enjoying some vacation time after running for vice president under James Cox, FDR and his kids sailed the scenic waters near Campobello Island. Afterwards, they had a swim in a nearby pond, and then he raced the kids back to the cottage. But it was when they returned to the cottage that Roosevelt began to feel odd, feverish, and more tired than usual.

He decided to skip dinner and go right to bed. "And he never walked without help again," says Biographer Geoffrey C. Ward. When he woke the next morning, he couldn't move his left leg, and then his right leg gave way. "I tried to persuade myself that the trouble with my leg was muscular," Roosevelt wrote later, "that it would disappear as I used it. But presently, it refused to work. And then the other."

Two days later, he lost the use of all his muscles from the chest down. He also had a high fever and pain in his neck and back. At 39 years old and with a promising political career ahead of him, Roosevelt was diagnosed with polio (poliomyelitis), a common disease at the time which can leave some muscles paralyzed, as was the case for FDR.

Acknowledging that he was permanently paralyzed did not dissuade Roosevelt from continuing to pursue his political career, which was remarkable for his time.

FDR built his own mobile chair by adding wheels to a small desk chair. This homemade device had a more familiar look and carried less of the stigma of a traditional wheelchair.

But the fact is FDR's disability only strengthened his determination and resolve. He was perhaps a better president as a result of his condition, as it taught him perseverance and gave him a sense of compassion and acceptance for those less fortunate.

And today, FDR serves as an inspiration for anyone with a physical disability to overcome. The only president to serve more than two terms, he saw the country through the Great Depression and World War II.

Thought for Today

What challenges are you facing today?

If you don't believe you can overcome a challenge, then you are defeated before you start. Today think about a challenge you are facing and see if you can approach it with a determined 'Can Do' approach. Don't let your negative inner voice talk you out of it. Start with some action (any action), and that will give you the momentum to continue.

Today's Reflection

_____

_____

_____

_____

_____

_____

_____

_____

_____

_____

_____

_____

IT'S ALL ABOUT PERSPECTIVE

"*You must try to keep your problems in perspective. You've probably heard the saying: 'I grumbled because I had no shoes, then I met a man who had no feet.'*

In a Peanuts cartoon, Snoopy looks in and sees the family sitting around the table, enjoying Thanksgiving dinner while he's outside eating dog food. 'How about that?' he thinks. 'Everybody's eating turkey today, but because I'm just a dog, I get dog food.'

Then he suddenly regains his perspective. 'Of course, things could be worse – I could have been born a turkey!'

How big or how difficult our problem appears to be is often a matter of perspective. Most difficulties we face are pretty insignificant in the larger scheme of things.

When a friend gets cancer, or you lose a loved one, we're reminded of just how petty our issues are. Author James Agee recalled how he once struck up a conversation with an impoverished elderly woman in the heart of Appalachia during the Great Depression.

She lived in a tiny shack with dirt floors, no heat, and no indoor plumbing. 'What would you do,' he asked, 'if someone gave you some money to help you out?'

The woman thought for a moment and answered, 'I guess I'd give it to the poor.'

Realising there are people around you who have much bigger problems than yours brings gratitude and perspective."

What a wonderful way to live. That woman was content with what she had in life – how amazing is that! She had nothing, yet she had everything. She turned down money to improve her life because she was happy with what she had and saw that others around her had less. She saw them as poor!

This is a great mindset and leads to a fulfilled, content, and happy life. It is not about the things in your life and how big your house is compared to others. It is not about how much money you have in the bank. It's about being grateful for what you have and caring for others.

Thought for Today

Do you realise you have the power to choose how you view your problems?

You can choose to change your perspective and see things differently. Today think about how you view things in your life. Are you grateful for what you have rather than envious of what you don't have? A wonderful way to live is to learn to be content in whatever season you are in. If you can learn to do this, you will live a great life.

Today's Reflection

_____

_____

_____

_____

_____

_____

_____

_____

_____

_____

_____

THE BUTTERFLY AND THE COCOON

"*One day, a small gap appeared in the cocoon, through which the butterfly had to appear. A boy, who accidentally passed by, stopped and watched how the butterfly was trying to get out of the cocoon.*

It took a lot of time, the butterfly was trying very hard, and the gap was as little as before. It seemed that the power would leave the butterfly soon.

The boy decided to help the butterfly. He took a penknife and cut the cocoon. The butterfly immediately got out, but its body was weak and feeble, and the wings were barely moving.

The boy continued to watch the butterfly, thinking that now its wings would spread, and it would fly. However, that did not happen. The rest of its life, the butterfly, had to drag its weak body and wings that weren't spread.

It was unable to fly because the boy did not realise that an effort to enter through the narrow gap of the cocoon was necessary for the butterfly so that the life-giving fluid would move from the body to the butterfly's wings and that the butterfly could fly.

Life forced the butterfly to leave its shell with difficulty so that it would become stronger and would be able to grow and develop.

If we were allowed to live without meeting difficulties, we would not be viable. Life gives us challenges to make us stronger.

Next time you are faced with a challenge, will you let the water sink your ship? Or will you let the water carry you to new destinations?"

There are often no shortcuts to life, and we need to go through certain processes to grow in the right way. We need to experience failure to develop a good resilient character; we can't develop this reading a book.

We have to go through the various stages of school in order to be ready to go to University. Without all the pain and stress of study and exams, we wouldn't be ready for the next level.

I believe that the only way we grow in our comfort zone and character is when we are under pressure. When things are going well, we rest and recover, and that is very important. But when the pressure is on - we grow.

Thought for Today

How do you view pressure - do you see it as positive or negative?

Pressure makes us stronger and better - think about this today and see what observations you make. Do you believe that we need to go through some pain in order to grow? Is it inevitable that we will face difficulties and hardships in life? If so, how we respond is crucial because if we embrace this principle, we will grow to accept it and benefit from it.

Today's Reflection

_____

_____

_____

_____

_____

_____

_____

_____

_____

THINKING OUT OF THE BOX
(CREATIVE THINKING)

*I*n a small Italian town, hundreds of years ago, a small business owner owed a large sum of money to a loan-shark. The loan-shark was a very old, unattractive looking guy that just so happened to fancy the business owner's daughter.

He decided to offer the businessman a deal that would completely wipe out the debt he owed him. However, the catch was that he would only wipe out the debt if he could marry the businessman's daughter.

Needless to say, this proposal was met with a look of disgust.

The loan-shark said that he would place two pebbles into a bag, one white and one black.

The daughter would then have to reach into the bag and pick out a pebble. If it were black, the debt would be wiped, but the loan-shark would then marry her. If it were white, the debt would also be wiped, but the daughter wouldn't have to marry the loan-shark.

Standing on a pebble-strewn path in the businessman's garden, the loan-shark bent over and picked up two pebbles. Whilst he was picking them up, the daughter noticed that he'd picked up two black pebbles and placed them both into the bag.

He then asked the daughter to reach into the bag and pick one.

The daughter naturally had three choices as to what she could have done:

Refuse to pick a pebble from the bag. Take both pebbles out of the bag and expose the loan-shark for cheating. Pick a pebble from the bag fully well, knowing it was black and sacrifice herself for her father's freedom.

She drew out a single pebble from the bag, and before looking at it, 'accidentally' dropped it into the midst of the other pebbles. She said to the loan-shark;

"Oh, how clumsy of me. Never mind, if you look into the bag for the one that is left, you will be able to tell which pebble I picked."

The pebble left in the bag was obviously black, and seeing as the loan-shark didn't want to be exposed, he had to play along as if the pebble the daughter dropped was white and clear her father's debt.

*It's always possible to **overcome a tough situation** through out of the box thinking, and not give in to the only options you think you have to pick from.*

Thought for Today

When you are faced with something difficult, take a step back to find other options.

Thinking outside the box pays real dividends. Today think of some problem you are facing and see if you can take a step back and spend some time just thinking of different solutions, which may be a little outside the box. When we do this, we sometimes stumble upon a solution which has eluded us. Take a step back to take two steps forward.

Today's Reflection

_____

_____

_____

_____

_____

_____

_____

_____

_____

_____

STEP BACK AND SEE THE BIGGER PICTURE

"*One day, the Chamber of Commerce in a small town invited a successful businessman to come and speak. The local economy was bad, and they were discouraged, so his job was to motivate them.*

He took a large piece of white paper and made a red dot in the centre of it. 'What do you see?' he asked the audience.

One person replied, 'I see a red dot.' The speaker said, 'Fine, but what else do you see?'

Others chimed in, 'A red dot.' The speaker asked, 'Don't you see anything else besides the dot?' He asked. The audience responded with a resounding 'no!'

The speaker said, 'You've overlooked the most important thing; you've missed seeing the sheet of paper!'

Then he went on to explain that in life, we are often distracted by small, dot-like failures and experiences.

They keep us from seeing the blessings and successes that are more important than the disappointments that try to monopolise our attention and drain our energy.

A poet once wrote, 'Two men looked through prison bars. One saw mud, the other stars.'

What are you looking at?

Are you so preoccupied with what is, that you've lost sight of what can be?"

Each day we experience negative things which appear in our day like dark dots. They could be a traffic jam, the children not getting ready for school, being late for a meeting, bad phone calls, or tough meetings at work.

If we focus on one of these dark dots, we experience negative feelings, usually fear or anger. These negative emotions change the way we feel very quickly, and we soon lose energy and feel down.

To change this, we need to see the bigger picture and focus on what is going well in our lives. As we do this, the positive emotions change the way we feel, and we experience higher energy levels and a feeling of positivity.

Thought for Today

Change your focus to the bigger picture and focus on what is going well in your life.

We can only think of one thing at a time, and our feelings are directly connected to our thoughts - so what you think, you feel. Today observe your feelings, and when you feel negative, check at that precise time what you are thinking about. See if that thought is negative. To change the way you feel think of something positive. As you do this, observe your improved energy levels and feelings.

Today's Reflection

_____

_____

_____

_____

_____

_____

_____

_____

_____

_____

SET GOALS TO ACHIEVE MORE

One day Supreme Court Justice Oliver Wendell Holmes lost his train ticket. As he searched for it, obviously irritated, the conductor said, 'It's okay, Your Honour; just mail it in. We all know you and trust you.' Holmes replied, 'I'm not concerned about finding my ticket – I just want to know where I'm going!'

Having goals lets you know where you're going in life. Fifty percent of the people around you have no idea where they're going. Another 40 percent will go in any direction they're led. The remaining 10 percent know where they'd like to go – but fewer than half of them are prepared to pay the price to get there.

Store owner J.C. Penney said, 'Give me a stock clerk with a goal, and I'll give you someone who'll make history. On the other hand, give me someone without a goal, and I'll give you a stock clerk.'

The truth is, while you are working on your goals, your goals are working on you. And the reward you get for reaching them isn't nearly as important as what you become in pursuit of them.

Goal setting is like a compass - you set it, then you head in that direction. A plane going 500mph without a destination will never get there no matter how fast it is going. You need to have a destination where you are heading in life; otherwise, you will just wander about.

At age 59, I thought that I'd missed my opportunity in life. I then discovered the principles of Mental Resilience and applied them to my life. I realised that I still had at least 20 years to change my life and set about doing just that.

I remember thinking just before things started to turn around that *I would never have another holiday as long as I lived, I would just about survive, then I would die.*

Over the following few years I met and married Julie who is one amazing woman, we have travelled to Dubai four times, Washington DC, San Diego, Germany, Finland four times, Poland, Switzerland, Malta, Gibraltar, Abu Dhabi, and Ireland. I stopped decorating six years ago, and the business is thriving.

Thought for Today

Do you have any goals in your life?

Today think about anything you would like to achieve as a goal. Research confirms that people who have written down goals achieve far more than those who don't. Spend some time today thinking about what you would love to do in the future and maybe who you would like to help or bless. When you have goals written down in words or in pictures, amazing things start to happen.

Today's Reflection

_____

_____

_____

_____

_____

_____

_____

_____

_____

_____

DON'T BE A BARNYARD CHICKEN, BE AN EAGLE!

There once was a hunter who found an abandoned eagle egg. Concerned for the life within, he brought the egg home to his farm and placed it with a few chicken eggs. In due time, the baby eagle hatched from its shell alongside a few chicks.

The baby-eagle began his life just like the chicks, sheltered by the mother hen. As the baby eagle matured, he ate, strutted, and even tried to 'cluck' and 'cackle' like a chicken.

One day as a bald eagle flew over the hunter's farm, he saw the little eagle mingling together with the other chickens. He flew down to talk to the young eagle. As the bald eagle landed, all the terrified chickens ran away. As the young eagle tried to run away, he was stopped by the bald eagle.

The bald eagle asked, 'What are you doing here among all these chickens? You are an eagle! You can fly, and your home is high up among the cliffs!' The young eagle was confused and could not accept the fact that he was an eagle. He responded, 'I can't fly, I am a chicken! This is where I belong, close to the ground!'

The bald eagle grabbed the young eagle in its claws and flew to a nearby cliff. As they rested on the cliff, the bald eagle said, 'You are an eagle, and you can fly!' and with a mighty swish of his wings, the bald eagle carried the young eagle up into the clouds.

Once they soared high above the clouds, the bald eagle dropped the young eagle as he yelled, 'Flap your wings and fly! You're an eagle!' To his bewilderment, the young eagle flapped his wings and discovered that he could fly.

We are all born eagles and have the potential to soar high above the clouds. However, many of us believe we are chickens and don't believe we can leave the ground. We all have a higher potential within. We need to help ourselves and others to realize it. Today become an eagle!

Thought for Today

What is your true potential?

Today think about your life and see if there are areas where you haven't fulfilled your potential. Perhaps like the confused eagle, you are trapped by your belief system. People may have told you limiting things about yourself, which are not true, but by believing them, you have made them real. Identify areas where you lack confidence and step out in faith.

Today's Reflection

_____

_____

_____

_____

_____

_____

_____

_____

_____

_____

Booker T. Washington:

"If you want to lift yourself up, lift up someone else."

DREAM KILLERS

"In 1975, a low-level Hewlett Packard engineer called Steve Wozniak, whom nobody had ever heard of, shared a dream with his pal, Steve Jobs. It was about building and selling an easy-to-use personal computer to the masses around the world.

The pair worked round the clock to create their compact PC. But when they offered it to Hewlett Packard, one of the world's great companies, the powers-that-be failed to see its incredible potential and gave it the thumbs down.

So, Wozniak and Jobs went off on their own and founded a little company called Apple Computers – and revolutionised the computer industry!

There's no shortage of people who will tell you, 'It can't be done' or 'It won't work.' There's a name for those people: 'dream killers' – and if you listen to them, you'll give up before you even begin.

Behind every major accomplishment, you'll find ordinary people with dreams, who are willing to take responsibility and risks. They are the people who enjoy the rewards!

Despite your failures, your struggles, and your limitations, if you're willing to disregard the naysayers, step out in faith, and use the gifts you have been given, you will see amazing things appear in your life."

The word Persistence springs to mind here. These two friends could have given up many times after they faced rejection after rejection, but they didn't. They believed in the idea they had, and the rest is history.

They showed a remarkable self-belief and just wouldn't take no for an answer. They ignored the negative people in their lives who said it couldn't be done, and they would end up regretting the risk they were taking.

Virtually every successful person in sport, business, music, dance, etc., have faced massive challenges where they wanted to give up, but they didn't. And because they didn't give up, they finally achieved the success they deserved and enjoyed for decades.

Thought for Today

How do you respond to negative people in your life?

Today think about the influence other people have on your life. Do you let what other people say about you become your reality? When you are faced with a challenge, do you allow the words of other people to set your direction? Do you really go for things, or do you give up after a while? Successful people keep going and eventually breakthrough.

Today's Reflection

_____

_____

_____

_____

_____

_____

_____

_____

_____

_____

_____

_____

NEAR FATAL CAR ACCIDENT

I will never forget the date of my accident; it was the 24th of June 2016, the day after the Brexit vote. That morning I had presented what was arguably the best Mental Resilience talk I have ever given to an appreciative business audience. The response was terrific, and the written feedback was even better. I also sold more books than I have ever sold at a single event. As you can imagine, I was incredibly happy.

When I set off back home, the sun was shining, and the road was clear. Then I had to slow right down as I saw a sign warning of a queue ahead and roadworks. The next thing I remember is my head hitting the airbag and extreme pain in my hips. I have two hip replacements, and this pain really concerned me. I also felt a searing pain in my spine, where I have a prolapsed disc. I bounced back off the airbag, and the force of my body hitting my seat caused the seat to break.

As I started to come round, shock set in and adrenaline shot through my body to help with the pain. Both airbags had activated, and my radio had come out of its housing. I can still see the smoke coming out of the airbags and the destruction around me.

The fire brigade cut the roof off my car, got me on a board, and six firemen lifted me out. I was rushed to Coventry hospital, where a team was waiting for me when I arrived. They were amazing. I had a full-body scan, and to my relief, there was no spinal damage, broken bones, or internal bleeding. For the next couple of weeks, it felt like I had been in a 12 round boxing match.

The car which hit me at about 70 mph was a medium-sized car – if it had been a larger car, a four-wheel drive, or lorry, then I may not be here to recount these events. I have come out of this well. My mindset is strong, and I am driving again, and to help reinforce my positive mindset, I wrote a list of all the things to be thankful for. I am grateful that I am alive, and I made a full recovery. I am grateful that the passengers in the other car survived. I am grateful that my car was replaced, and my life goes on.

Thought for Today

It's not what happens to you, but how you respond.

How do you respond when things go wrong? Today
think about this phrase: 'There is always a seed of
something positive in every negative situation.'
See if you can find something positive in a negative
situation you face today. When you do this, you
will realise that something positive came out of this
situation and you will feel better.

Today's Reflection

_____

_____

_____

_____

_____

_____

_____

_____

_____

_____

_____

THE GROUP OF FROGS

"*As a group of frogs was traveling through the woods, two of them fell into a deep pit. When the other frogs crowded around the pit and saw how deep it was, they told the two frogs that there was no hope left for them.*

However, the two frogs decided to ignore what the others were saying, and they proceeded to try and jump out of the pit.

Despite their efforts, the group of frogs at the top of the pit were still saying that they should just give up. That they would never make it out.

Eventually, one of the frogs took heed to what the others were saying, and he gave up, falling down to his death. The other frog continued to jump as hard as he could. Again, the crowd of frogs yelled at him to stop the pain and just die.

He jumped even harder and finally made it out. When he got out, the other frogs said, "Did you not hear us?"

The frog explained to them that he was deaf. He thought they were encouraging him the entire time.

People's words can have a significant effect on other people. Think about what you say before it comes out of your mouth. It might just be the difference between life and death.

Your words can either build people up or destroy them, so choose what you say carefully. You may remember a teacher who made you feel small, and since then, you have lacked confidence in public places. Or it could be a parent who told you that you are stupid and will never amount to anything in life. It could be some friends who made fun of you and laughed at you. Or it could be a school bully who taunted you in school and left you scarred mentally.

The words we hear are critically important. If we experience positive words as we grow up, we will grow up healthy and happy. If we experience negative words, we will grow up damaged, broken, and carrying mental scars which affect our future in a powerful way.

Thought for Today

What sort of words did you hear as you were growing up?

Today think about the impact of encouragement and how you can use that to help others. You may have experienced real negativity from significant others, but that doesn't mean you can't encourage others. Make it your mission to encourage as many people as you can and observe the impact these words have. When you do this, you will be impacted too.

Today's Reflection

_____

_____

_____

_____

_____

_____

_____

_____

_____

_____

LEAVE A LEGACY

"*You don't get to choose the moment of your arrival and departure here on earth, but you get to choose what your legacy will be, what you will be remembered for. At five, he wrote an advanced concerto for the harpsichord.*

Before he was ten, he published several violin sonatas and was playing the best of Handel and Bach from memory. Soon after his twelfth birthday, he composed and conducted his first opera.

He was awarded an honorary appointment as concertmaster with the Salzburg Symphony Orchestra, and within a few years, was hailed as the pride of Salzburg. When he died at age thirty-five, he had written forty-eight symphonies; forty-seven arias, duets, and quartets, with orchestral accompaniment; and more than a dozen operas.

Who was this amazing man? It was Wolfgang Amadeus Mozart. He's credited with some 600 original compositions in all. Even so, Mozart lived most of his life in poverty and died in obscurity. His sick widow seemed indifferent about his death. A few friends made it to the church for his funeral, but a storm prohibited their going to the graveside for his burial.

So the location of his grave became virtually impossible to identify. No shrine marks his resting place. Today, what is Mozart remembered for? What is his legacy? Not the life he lived, but the music he gave the world that still enriches our lives.

When your life's sole focus is self-interest, you won't be missed when you are gone or missed for the right reasons. So, find a cause greater than yourself, one that will outlive you, and pour yourself into it.

Don't just leave a will, leave a legacy that makes a real difference. What a wonderful way to live your life knowing that you have fulfilled your purpose in life.

Experts say that finding your purpose and then living it out is the most beautiful existence. You get up each morning with a skip in your step, knowing that what you are doing will impact future generations in some way.

Thought for Today

Will what you are doing outlive you and leave a legacy?

When you live for something greater than yourself, you feel something beautiful. Today see if you can think of something where you leave a legacy. It could be your children who you have brought up. It could be some impact you have had on another human being. It could be a charity you set up. What do you want to be remembered for?

Today's Reflection

_____

_____

_____

_____

_____

_____

_____

_____

_____

_____

STAY IN THE GAME

"*Author Jon Gordon says: 'There was a time, as children, when we jumped from the jungle gym and went on roller coaster rides. No goal was unattainable. Then, when we grew up, the doubters dissuaded us from going after our dreams.*

"You're crazy…it's too hard…play it safe…dreams weren't meant for people like us." They instilled their insecurities in us…and with so many people saying we can't…and so few saying we can, we let fear into our lives.

We're so scared of losing what we have that we don't go after what we want. We hold on so tightly to the status quo that we never experience what could be…I call this "playing to lose". We see it in sports.

When a team has the lead, they start thinking about how not to lose instead of how to win. They play safe and scared while the other team takes chances, plays without fear, and wins.

Adopt a "play to win" mindset…one that says even if you do fail, you won't give up or let your dreams die. Success isn't automatically given to us; it's pursued with all the energy and sweat we can muster.

Obstacles and struggles are part of life…they make us appreciate success. If everything came easy, we'd never know how it feels to succeed. Obstacles were meant to be overcome.

Fear was meant to be conquered. Success was meant to be achieved. They're part of life, and those who succeed refuse to give up till the game is over."

This is a great way to live life – taking on the challenges in life and overcoming them. If we see the difficulties we face as part of life, we won't get downhearted when they appear, and we will have the energy and motivation to take them on.

Thought for Today

How do you feel about the obstacles you face daily?

Obstacles are meant to be overcome. Do you see them as a hindrance and negative or a challenge to overcome? If we view them as a challenge, we create a different mindset, and the outcome is better. Rather than shutting down, we rise up to take on the challenge. Try using the word Challenge instead of Problem and see how your mindset changes.

Today's Reflection

_____

_____

_____

_____

_____

_____

_____

_____

_____

_____

_____

HARD WORK AND INTEGRITY

*I*n 'The Finishing Touch,' author Chuck Swindoll tells about a man he met who made a great impression on him:

'With a grin and a twinkle, he whipped out his hand. It was a hand you could strike a match on, toughened by decades of rugged toil.

"You look like a man who enjoys life. What do you do for a living?" I asked.

"Me? Well, I'm a farmer from back in the Midwest." Swindoll asked him, "What did you do last week?" He said, "Last week, I finished harvesting ninety thousand bushels of corn." I then blurted out, "Ninety thousand! How old are you, my friend?"

He didn't seem at all hesitant or embarrassed by my question. "I'm just a couple of months shy of ninety." He laughed again as I shook my head.

He had lived through four wars, the Great Depression, sixteen presidents, ninety Midwest winters, who knows how many personal hardships, and he was still taking life by the throat. I had to ask him the secret of his long and productive life.

"Hard work and integrity" was his quick reply. As we parted company, he looked back over his shoulder and added, "Don't take it easy, young feller. Stay at it!"

Hard work and integrity!

Those two qualities go together and are the essence of a life well-lived. And when you practise them faithfully, you experience the highest level of joy and fulfilment in life.'

How do you view hard work and integrity? This is worth spending some time thinking about. Experts say that there is no shortcut to hard work, but the great news is that you can learn to enjoy the process. I love the feeling when I have worked really hard, and I finish for the day. I have a great feeling of satisfaction as I eat my supper and watch a box set. There is something very satisfying about achieving something through hard work.

Thought for Today

Embrace hard work, and see how you can start to enjoy it.

Do you give it your all, or do you just do enough to get by? Today think about your work ethic and also your integrity. Does integrity matter? Is it important to be honest and trustworthy? If you work diligently, there is a feeling of satisfaction, which simply makes you feel good. See if you can think of anything which you can apply to your life.

Today's Reflection

_____

_____

_____

_____

_____

_____

_____

_____

_____

_____

DON'T MISS YOUR OPPORTUNITY

"*Guess which big company felt like 'choking on its own chocolate' after it elected not to feature one of its products in the 1982 blockbuster film E.T.?*

If you said M&M's, you'd be right! How did it happen? It turns out the Mars chocolate bar company executives decided nothing could be gained from allowing their M&M's sweets to be used in what some of them considered 'a silly movie.'

Consequently, the little boy Elliott ended up luring the loveable alien E.T. with Hershey's Reese's Pieces. That one scene drew millions of customers worldwide into sweet shops in quest of Reese's Pieces!

Thanks to this movie mega-hit, Hershey's sales shot up 65 percent! It's interesting that the Mars executives who said 'No' probably lived in big houses, drove big cars, and earned big salaries!

Yep, doubt and fear stalk the rich as well as the poor; you'll find naysayers at the top and bottom of the corporate ladder.

Do you recall these words from the famous poem by John Greenleaf Whittier: 'For of all sad words of tongue or pen, the saddest are these, "It might have been"'?

Think of all the times opportunity knocked, and nobody answered.

Are you standing before a door of opportunity today? Are you afraid to walk through it? Don't be. Take courage and believe that the best is yet to come."

As Henry Ford once famously said: "If you think you Can or think you Can't, you are right either way."

We can choose how we respond to fear and risk. We can choose negative or positive. If we choose negative, we will turn opportunity away – if we choose positive, we will have a chance of something great appearing in our lives.

Taking risks can be reckless, I am not advocating taking every risk which comes along but to consider each one and to take the challenge to step out when one of these risks 'feels' right.

Most of the things which happen to us are a result of our thinking – it all starts inside our mind then appears in our lives. We can change our circumstances by changing the way we think, speak, and act.

Thought for Today

Calculated risks can open up amazing doors for you.

Today think about the risks you do or don't take. Taking calculated risks isn't for everyone, but for those who do take them, life is more exciting – and scary. Being scared and excited isn't meant to be for all and sundry, but for the right people, it's a great way to live. If you want to see what you are made of, take a small risk or two, and see what happens. Start by taking small risks, then build from there.

Today's Reflection

_____

_____

_____

_____

_____

_____

_____

_____

_____

_____

_____

LIVING A HAPPY AND CONTENT LIFE

"*One morning, a businessman saw a fisherman lounging on his boat drinking coffee. 'You're back early,' he shouted. The sailor replied, 'I've caught enough. I'm through for the day.'*

The businessman said, 'Why not go out again? If you keep going out, you can catch more fish and increase your income, buy a second boat, hire a crew, and become rich like me.'

The man replied, 'Why should I do that?' The businessman said, 'So you'll be free to do what you want and enjoy life.'

Grinning, the fisherman said, 'But that's exactly what I'm doing right now!'

Wise people say, 'Be satisfied with what you have,' yet many of us base our self-worth on what we own or achieve.

We only feel good about ourselves when we're involved in certain relationships or live in certain areas or reach certain goals. We tell ourselves, 'When I earn more money, or become CEO, or get fitter, etc., I'll be okay.'

So, what's the basis of your self-worth today? If you're not sure, ask yourself, 'What can I not live without?' Is there somebody you're afraid will leave you? A job you're too involved in?

Is there something you need to accomplish before you feel complete? It is wise to have goals for your life, but don't undermine yourself by believing that you're 'less than' because you've achieved or acquired less than someone else."

I used to be just like this, always striving for perfection and being the best. I never achieved perfection or the best, and I was always insecure and incomplete. I am now grateful for everything I currently have and grateful for what I am achieving. I don't have to be perfect, and I don't have to be the best.

Living a happy, content, and fulfilled life is what most people strive for. You don't have to be a millionaire to achieve this, but you can be content with everything around you and within you. You can have all areas of your life in balance, and you can have peace and joy in your heart. You can be grateful for everything you have as well as the people close to you. This is what I call living a good life.

Thought for Today

What are you striving for?

Today think about your life and what you are trying to achieve. Are you happy with the direction you are heading? Are you trying too hard to keep up with the 'Jones's'? Think about what is really important to you and check how you are doing in relation to that. Are you on target to live a content and fulfilled life? If not, what can you do about it?

Today's Reflection

_____

_____

_____

_____

_____

_____

_____

_____

_____

_____

_____

_____

STRESS PARALYSES YOU

"*O*nce upon a time, a psychology professor walked around on a stage while teaching stress management principles to an auditorium filled with students.

As she raised a glass of water, everyone expected they'd be asked the typical 'glass half empty or glass half full' question. Instead, with a smile on her face, the professor asked,

'How heavy is this glass of water I'm holding?'

Students shouted out answers ranging from eight ounces to a couple of pounds.

She replied, 'From my perspective, the absolute weight of this glass doesn't matter. It all depends on how long I hold it.

If I hold it for a minute or two, it's fairly light. If I hold it for an hour straight, its weight might make my arm ache a little.

If I hold it for a day straight, my arm will likely cramp up and feel completely numb and paralyzed, forcing me to drop the glass to the floor.

In each case, the weight of the glass doesn't change, but the longer I hold it, the heavier it feels to me.'

As the class nodded their heads in agreement, she continued, 'Your stresses and worries in life are very much like this glass of water.

Think about them for a while, and nothing happens. Think about them a bit longer, and you begin to ache a little.

Think about them all day long, and you will feel completely numb and paralyzed – incapable of doing anything else until you drop them.'"

Stress is recognised by many as the number one proxy killer disease today. We can't ignore the effects of stress across the world and the impact it is having on every single person. This is a time to stay calm and keep positive, believing that there are better days ahead.

We can only think of one thing at a time. Whenever you feel stress, it is a result of your thoughts being focussed on something negative. To change the way you feel, switch your focus onto something positive, and you will start to feel better. Do this regularly. Make it a habit, and you will start the process of reducing stress in your life.

Thought for Today

It's better not to spend time worrying about things you have no control over.

. Today observe how many times you worry about things which concern you. Do you spend a lot of time doing this? Do you worry about the future or things in the past? When you are stressed, you are damaging your body. To release the stress, think of something which makes you happy and focus on that. Then take some action and move on.

Today's Reflection

_____

_____

_____

_____

_____

_____

_____

_____

_____

_____

_____

IT'S NOT ALL BAD

Whardhen I started this journey of blogs nearly ten years ago, I couldn't have predicted that the very last of my 100 favourite stories would end up being influenced by a pandemic of global proportions, changing the way we think, live, and work possibly forever.

I wanted to end with something positive and something related to what we are all going through, and if you are reading this years from now, hopefully it will be even more poignant.

I am so pleased to share with you the following article from Forbes Magazine that will hopefully inspire you.

I have always said that "There is a seed of something positive in every negative situation."

Forbes Magazine

"The coronavirus is deadly serious. It's wreaking havoc for individuals, companies, municipalities, and the world. The news is filled with stories of sickness, job loss, disappointment, and death. There's no shortage of bad news when it comes to COVID-19.

It is impacting our ability to be productive and engaged in our work. Exposure to all this negativity is making even the most optimistic among us feel frustrated, deflated, and even depressed.

*Making matters worse, this **negativity is highly contagious**. We're taking significant precautions to protect our physical health, so why do we resist protecting ourselves from things that can harm our mental health? Part of the reason comes from a built-in negativity bias we human beings possess.*

In the field of psychology (and defined in Wikipedia) negativity bias is "the notion that even when of equal intensity, things of a more negative nature (e.g., unpleasant thoughts, emotions, or social interactions; harmful/ traumatic events) have a greater effect on one's psychological state and processes than neutral or positive things."

*So the way to override that primal alarm (which now does us more harm than good) is to drown it out with things that are positive, heart-warming, and encouraging. One study suggests **we need at least five times as many positive stimuli to counteract the negative.***

Now's the time to fill your heart and mind with all things fun, optimistic, and kind. When we look for them, there are many positives to these otherwise tumultuous times. You just have to be intentional about it. These four ways, along with some examples, are a good start.

Humanity

*Focus on the stories that remind you of the **goodness of humanity** and the power of **human connection**. In Rome, on Friday, March 13th, everyone was encouraged to go open their windows or go out on their balconies to play music and sing. It prompted the hashtag #EverythingWillBeFine.*

A North Carolina woman wanted to share her engagement with her grandfather, who was in a nursing home that did not allow visitors. She found a way to show him the ring by pressing her hand to his window.

Time

Time may be the greatest gift of this devasting crisis. If you are now working from home, you've just been gifted your commute time. If some of your work is postponed or cancelled, or if you've unfortunately been furloughed or even laid off, you surely have less wealth, but you do have more time.

*How can you spend that time in a way that will bring you joy **and happiness**—now and for the future? Back when you were working overtime and longed for a break, who were you missing? What did you wish you could do in order to restore the balance in your life?*

*Fill your time with **reaching out to people** you love or dabbling in things you have always wanted to try. Learn a language. Reconnect with old friends. Develop a new meditation habit.*

Generosity

*Human beings are wired to be generous. And **being generous is good for your health**. When you give, you increase your self-esteem and self-worth. It also gives your immune system a boost.*

*Oprah magazine highlighted a story that showed that "simply c**ontemplating generosity boosts your immunity**. When Harvard students watched a film about Mother Teresa tending to orphans, the number of protective antibodies in their saliva surged."*

So help those who need it, and share in the positive benefits for yourself. The stories of doing good could fill a library. NBA basketball stars are paying the salaries of the stadium workers who no longer have stadiums to staff.

Delta's CEO is giving up his salary to help keep workers paid during a crisis that is having a disproportionate impact on travel industry workers. TV shows Grey's Anatomy, The Good Doctor, and The Resident have decided to donate their show wardrobe—surgical gloves and medical gowns—to the real doctors and medical professionals who need them.

Doing good doesn't require fame or privilege; generosity is even more infectious than the disease itself. **Ordinary citizens are getting in on the act.** *The San Francisco Chronicle shined the spotlight on Sharky Laguana, the owner of Bandago, a San Francisco small business that rents vans. Laguana is working with City Hall to offer free use of his vans to transport homeless people to shelters or whatever else is needed.*

Humour

It may seem hard to find the humour in such a widespread, devasting crisis, but there's humour all around if you pay attention. According to mental health and wellness experts, **"Laughter relaxes your body, boosts the immune system, triggers the release of endorphins, protects the heart, and burns calories."**

The next time you want to check for another crisis update online, reach for something funny instead. Stop feeding your mind a diet of doom. Check out funny clips on YouTube, watch a comedy, or a comedy box set.

Laugh. Give. Appreciate. Acknowledge. Support. Reduce the negativity and lift your spirits to new heights."

A healthier planet

Another unexpected side effect of coronavirus is the positive impact on the environment. The canals of Venice, normally filled with pollution from people and boat traffic, recovered. They're now sparkling with sea life, including **dolphins.**

And the sky is clearer over much of the world, thanks to fewer cars on the road and aircraft in the sky. The planet is recovering.

Thought for Today

Seek out stories of humanity and the good that people are doing.

Today on the last day of this book, think about all the good things in the world and how you can make it a better place. Who can you help, who can you call, who can you encourage? I really believe that the true way to happiness is helping others. It is for no personal gain in any way. It is simply a gesture of love to lift someone and to make their day brighter.

Today's Reflection

_____

_____

_____

_____

_____

_____

_____

_____

_____

_____

_____

SUMMARY

Congratulations, you've done it! 100 days, 100 stories, 100 insights into how people have used the power of mental resilience to overcome adversity or see things in a different way to drive a better outcome or change their lives.

I hope you have found the book to be as inspirational as I did, putting it together for you. I trust you found a pace that worked well for you and that you have managed to make some real changes to how you can control your thoughts and therefore, your feelings.

This book can be a constant resource, a journal of notes and reminders for you to come back to time and time again.

In conclusion, I will leave you with the 12 Key Principles of Mental Resilience, which have helped to transform my life as well as thousands of other lives.

THE 12 KEY PRINCIPLES OF MENTAL RESILIENCE

1. The conscious mind can only think of one thing at a time; it flicks from one thing to another. When you think of something positive, you cannot, at the same time, think of something negative.

2. Your thoughts are directly connected to your feelings, so what you focus on is what you feel. To change your feeling, simply change your thinking.

3. When you focus on positive things, you have more energy. When you focus on negative things, you have less energy. When you are positive, you achieve more.

4. To change from negative thinking to positive thinking, simply recite in your mind everything you are grateful for. Because your mind can only think of one thing at a time, and your feelings are directly connected to your thoughts, you will start to feel better.

5. Worldwide evidence demonstrates that there is a direct connection between positive thinking and health. The more positive you are, the more likely it is you will be healthier.

6. There is a seed of something positive in every negative situation. Look for it, and you will find it. When you do

this, you will experience relief realising that something positive came out of the negative situation, which is a positive outcome.

7. The only time you grow in your comfort zone and character is when you are under pressure. Embrace pressure situations knowing that you are growing through the process.

8. Rest and recovery are crucial to a healthy, happy life. Make sure you rest and recover adequately.

9. Your Inner Voice either makes you or breaks you. Make sure you have developed a positive inner voice to help you perform well under pressure.

10. Your highest energy levels are in the morning, so schedule your most important tasks during this time. When your energy levels are high, you achieve more.

11. Sleep and good health are directly connected. Most people need 7-9 hours per night. When we sleep, our minds and bodies heal and rebuild, which results in better health.

12. Visualisation can help you achieve your dreams. Visualising your goals increases your focus and awareness of these dreams, which improves the chance of them appearing in your life.

Did you enjoy reading
100 DAYS to MENTAL RESILIENCE?

Maybe you would like to grab a copy of my 5* Best-Selling Book on Amazon.
'OFF THE WALL'

This is a self-help, easy to read handbook of tips and techniques for personal development; including mental resilience, self-confidence, public speaking, inner voice, positive mindset, stress management, inner chimp, reframing, belief system, law of attraction, visualisation, dream board, gratitude, mindfulness, energy levels, and sleep.

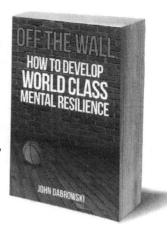

Using this book will help you positively change the way you think, speak, and act.

You will learn how to become more mentally resilient in all situations. You will be able to achieve more in your life by changing your belief system.

Learn to relax and enjoy living in the present moment. Stay energised through healthy eating and sleeping habits.

Here are some of the 38 x 5-star reviews OFF THE WALL has received on Amazon...

***** 5 STAR An Outstanding Book on Mental Resilience
"John's book contains many golden keys, which you can use to unlock and to resolve any problem in your life."

***** 5 STAR Learn how to survive & thrive, growing from everything life throws at you
"I can heartily recommend John Dabrowski's teachings, and this book is a great place to start."

***** 5 STAR A great "must read " book
"Strongly recommended for everyone who needs a little help to get to where they want to be in life."

***** 5 STAR Great messages for living your life
"Saw the author speak on Cunard cruise to New York. Very inspiring".

***** 5 STAR The Power of Visualisation
"I've read quite a few self-help books over the years, and they're all on my bookshelf, but this is the one I always dip into now so I would most definitely recommend it."

***** 5 STAR An essential toolkit for everyone!
"...read this book, which has really helped me get through the current Covid-19 lockdown having been placed on the job retention scheme. This was perfect timing, and I regularly practice the different techniques John provides."

***** 5 STAR Highly recommended
"This book has given me an excellent toolkit to work on my mental resilience, which I hope will benefit my career and personal life in the future. I would recommend this book to anyone who wants to understand and improve their mental resilience".

***** 5 STAR A great read
Off the Wall is not only an inspiring story about John and his life but packed full of tips and techniques to get so much more out of your own life. I certainly know how powerful the dream board and visualisation techniques are - I have tried and tested this out for myself, and it works. John's words, "What you see and what you say is what you get." I would agree with that, totally. A great read for getting the most out of your life as only you can achieve it.

***** 5 STAR Totally Inspiring
"I would urge anybody or group to purchase his book or book him as a headline speaker.

After suffering redundancy & several knocks this year I often referred to John's book for resilience advice; it has helped me secure a new position in the sector I work.
John is a brilliant example and inspiration."

***** 5 STAR I think the book is excellent It is well laid out and very easy to read
"I have read other self-help books but have come to the conclusion that if there was one book that covered most of

what you need to know, this is amongst the best. I consider it my bible."

…these are just some examples of the 5-star reviews OFF THE WALL has received on Amazon.

Just search for me by name, and please make sure you leave me a review of the book if you get the chance to read it.

You can also find out more about me and my Mental Resilience Masterclasses, Coaching, Training, and Keynote Speaking Engagements at www.jdmindcoach.com.

CONNECT WITH ME:
LinkedIn: linkedin.com/johndabrowski
Twitter:@jdmindcoach
Facebook: facebook.com/jdmindcoach
Email: john@jdmindcoach.co.uk

About the Author

John Dabrowski is the founder of JD Mindcoach Ltd, a company that helps individuals and organisations develop world-class Mental Resilience. John has experienced great challenges and adventures in his life, from being the last pick 'off the wall' at school, to playing basketball for England in the Commonwealth games.

He played basketball from the age of 12 and quickly improved by using the techniques of Mental Resilience that he discovered and developed. This led him into a professional basketball career where he played all over Europe, culminating in winning the Play-Off finals at Wembley live on BBC TV. In his latter playing days, he scored a British record of 98 points in a single match, which he credits to 'being in the zone.'

Following a serious back injury, he finished playing after the Play-Off victory and took up the position of Commercial Manager at Sunderland basketball club. It was here that he discovered a hidden talent for sales and marketing. He then became General Manager of the Manchester Giants basketball club, where with hard work and good management, they were voted the best-promoted club in England by the English Basketball Association.

John then left the basketball world to enter the sales arena, initially in the capacity of regional sales executive for the Metro Radio station in Newcastle. He quickly established himself in the role and was soon promoted to regional sales manager, where he flourished. He brought in record sales for the station, as well as hitting a record 19 monthly sales targets in a row.

Over the next 30 years, he worked for some outstanding design and advertising agencies, where he learned excellent sales and marketing techniques. He reached director level and won various national accounts as well as looking after large key accounts. He learned great rapport-building techniques, which helped him build his client base.

A few years ago, before he set up JD Mindcoach Ltd, he qualified as an NLP (Neuro-Linguistic Programming) practitioner and coach and completed various courses in Human Relations and Guided Imagery. He has attended many courses to develop his skills and is a member of the Professional Speaking Association.

John is an international speaker, a best-selling author, and expert on Mental Resilience. He delivers Mental Resilience Masterclasses both online and face to face and speaks around the world to various sized organisations, including Rolls Royce, Deloitte, Aviva, Hilton, Cunard, Nat West Bank, and the NHS.

He has spoken in Dubai four times, Finland four times, the USA three times; once was in San Diego where he spoke at the same conference as Barack Obama. Germany three times, Ireland twice, Poland, Switzerland, Malta, and Gibraltar.

He has also spoken at an international conference in Stockholm, Sweden. He has spoken three times on the Queen Mary 2 on a cruise to New York and is signed up to five speaking agencies.

John is 66 years of age with a plan to be still speaking on stage at the age of 80 – he believes that when you boil life down to a core statement, the following phrase he uses sums it all up:

**"It's not how you start in life that counts,
but how you finish!"**

Mental Resilience Masterclasses

John's unique Mental Resilience Masterclasses, both face to face and online, are having a big impact on the people attending. They are fun and interactive with great take away value. The life-transforming techniques are beneficial to both business and personal life. The new positive mindset developed creates renewed energy, resulting in a much-improved performance.

There are both half-day and full-day courses available, which take the attendees on a journey of self-discovery. The result of going through these is the ability to handle higher pressure, feel much more positive, and experience greater achievement.

Testimonials

"John is an amazing trainer, and he shared remarkable techniques on how to develop Mental Resilience. The human mind is a powerful tool, and 'Mental Resilience' is a power practice, which helps us remain committed and accomplish our goals in life."
Ms. Sangeeta Tewar, Human Resources Manager, British University in Dubai

"We really liked his story-telling skills, the clever use of media (short films, PowerPoint and interactive practice sessions), and the humoristic tone of his talk. The audience was enthused and ready to change their mindset! After

the event, we received really good feedback from the
participants, and as evidence of his success, John ran out of
books to sign!"

Marie Gow, Department for International Trade,
British Embassy, Switzerland

Listening to John reminded me about the importance of
wellbeing. His examples and anecdotes from his life made
me realise we are all on a very similar journey. The sooner
we learn how to live better and healthier, the better for our
work and personal lives. John's examples were simple yet so
powerful. John, thank you for a fantastic and eye-opening
talk."

Marta Zaremba-Marsden, IT Project Manager,
Rolls-Royce plc

John hosted the Masterclass on Zoom, and he started by
telling his story, which then led nicely into sharing several
techniques for managing our mental health and well-being
during this time of change. It was very informative and
thought provoking. There were some excellent lessons on
home working, especially as some of the team are working
from home. Everyone thoroughly enjoyed the session, and
we have the second Masterclass in two weeks' time. I would
highly recommend John and this Masterclass."

Peter Dawson, Head of Group Integrity, Samworth Brothers
(Soreen & Ginsters)

Keynote Talks

John has a truly unique style of presentation, which is inspiring thousands of people across the world. He has been described as authentic, honest, gifted, and totally inspirational. He has spoken to audiences across the world with consistently positive feedback. He uses his basketball sporting background to great effect when illustrating business situations.

One of the things that really inspires people is that John is a living example of the content he delivers in his talks. He is 66 years of age and has a 14-year plan to be speaking on stage at the age of 80 – few people doubt this will happen! During his life, he has faced many challenges: being the last off the wall in PE, not being able to speak English at the age of five, and not having the confidence to introduce a Professor to four students. Yet he has overcome all of these with techniques he shares in his talks.

Testimonials

"It was a pleasure to participate in John's presentation on mental resilience. The Hilton corporate HR group in McLean, Virginia, USA, enjoyed the presentation very much and appreciated the helpful, practical examples and reminders on how to build mental resilience!"

**Kimo Kippen, Vice President,
Global Workforce Initiatives, Hilton USA**

"On the back of a client recommendation, the bank invited John Dabrowski to speak at the 2016 Legal Conference series hosted in London, Edinburgh, and Manchester. John delivered a powerful, energetic, and insightful presentation on developing mental resilience. The subject resonated with the 300 strong audience of lawyers and legal firm managers."

Steve Arundale, Head of Commercial Professional Sectors.

NatWest Bank

"He taught us techniques on mental resilience, staying positive, and also how to relax. Feedback from the staff was overwhelmingly positive – he's an engaging guy with a fantastic story. I would not hesitate to recommend John as an inspirational speaker."

Douglas Barrett, Director for Trade and Investment,

British Embassy, Abu Dhabi

"John delivered a Mental Resilience session to our GPs and Practice nurses. I've never seen them so spellbound! You could hear a pin drop. John's style is personable, easy, and honest. He relates his own experience to the theories that he offers, which brings them alive for the audience. Importantly for healthcare professionals, he refers to evidence base where it exists and touches on some of the science behind the words. The feedback that we got from the session was incredibly positive."

Laura Sherburn, Chief Executive, Primary Care Doncaster

Executive Coaching

The vast experience John has in the business and sporting world gives him a unique coaching style, which is appreciated by his wide range of executive clients. He uses various NLP techniques as well as good old-fashioned listening skills to help his client 'see the wood for the trees.' There is something unique about a totally confidential coaching session where absolutely nothing is shared with anyone; there is 100% confidentiality. This provides a safe environment for complete honesty and openness, which brings about amazing solutions to challenges faced by the clients.

The sessions are powerful and result in the client taking action plans forward together with great levels of accountability to get things done.

Testimonials

"I have had numbers of coaching sessions with great coaches who had lots of credible training during the last decades, but no one has given me such practical tools and helpful nuggets of wisdom. You are by far the best coach that I ever had even though I have worked with a number of the most qualified coaches with great credentials. Your coaching gave me an insight that I am grateful to you forever."

Helen, Senior Manager NHS England

"Through coaching sessions John has a very simple message: choose the positive and let it transform your life. One of the outcomes is I have changed my diet and increased my fitness regime with the result that I am energised and feel great! His positivity is infectious, and will I know transform my role as a CEO."

Tim Desmond, CEO, The National Justice Museum

"I'm so grateful to John for his help to develop the mental resilience to overcome my own self-doubt to deliver my first public speech at a conference. Had I not had the coaching from John, I know that the nerves would have got the better of me, but with his techniques, I stayed positive all the way through. Thank you so much for your help. I have no boundaries now, and that is thanks to your great coaching."

**Vatsana Gordon, Head of Workforce Management,
HomeServe**

"I hired John to help me with the start-up phase of my new business. Having sold a business and started again, I felt I needed some personal backup to keep me going when things got tough, and so I see John every 2 weeks for personal coaching. Having John on the team has made a massive difference to my resilience, mind-set, and outlook, and as a result, I am getting so much more done and seeing opportunities everywhere. I would recommend John without hesitation to anyone wanting to achieve more with their life."

**Serena Humphries FCMA CGMA Director,
F Word Training Ltd**

ACTION PLAN for Mental Resilience.

By now, you might well be focused and fired up to get an action plan in place after reading 100 inspirational stories about Mental Resilience.

If you are anything like me, you might do better with a plan: a committed, written plan of action. Well, for those of you that feel you would need something like that, I've put together 10 pages for just that reason: An Action Plan.

I've made it simple to complete and easy to come back to and track your progress.

ACTION 1.

Point/Name/Theme

_____

What story really resonated with me?

_____

What was it about it that I liked?

_____

_____

What do I want to change in my life relating to this?

_____

_____

When do I want that change to start?

_____

_____

What impact will this change have on my life?

_____

_____

"No one can make you feel inferior without your consent."
– Eleanor Roosevelt

ACTION 2.

Point/Name/Theme

_____

What story really resonated with me?

_____

What was it about it that I liked?

_____

_____

What do I want to change in my life relating to this?

_____

_____

When do I want that change to start?

_____

_____

What impact will this change have on my life?

_____

_____

"It's not who you are that holds you back;
it's who you think you're not."
– Unknown

ACTION 3.

Point/Name/Theme

_____

What story really resonated with me?

_____

What was it about it that I liked?

_____

_____

What do I want to change in my life relating to this?

_____

_____

When do I want that change to start?

_____

_____

What impact will this change have on my life?

_____

_____

*"What the mind of man can conceive and believe,
the mind of man can achieve."*
– Napoleon Hill

ACTION 4.

Point/Name/Theme

_____

What story really resonated with me?

_____

What was it about it that I liked?

_____

_____

What do I want to change in my life relating to this?

_____

_____

When do I want that change to start?

_____

_____

What impact will this change have on my life?

_____

_____

"There are no accidents;
there is only some purpose that we haven't yet understood."
–Deepak Chopra

ACTION 5.

Point/Name/Theme

_____

What story really resonated with me?

_____

What was it about it that I liked?

_____

_____

What do I want to change in my life relating to this?

_____

_____

When do I want that change to start?

_____

_____

What impact will this change have on my life?

_____

_____

"Be miserable. Or motivate yourself. Whatever has to be done, it's always your choice."
– Wayne Dyer

ACTION 6.

Point/Name/Theme

_____

What story really resonated with me?

_____

What was it about it that I liked?

_____

_____

What do I want to change in my life relating to this?

_____

_____

When do I want that change to start?

_____

_____

What impact will this change have on my life?

_____

_____

"Twenty years from now you will be more disappointed by the things that you didn't do than by the ones you did do. Explore. Dream. Discover."
– Mark Twain

ACTION 7.

Point/Name/Theme

_____

What story really resonated with me?

_____

What was it about it that I liked?

_____

_____

What do I want to change in my life relating to this?

_____

_____

When do I want that change to start?

_____

_____

What impact will this change have on my life?

_____

_____

"People often say that motivation doesn't last. Well, neither does bathing – that's why we recommend it daily."
– Zig Ziglar

ACTION 8.

Point/Name/Theme

_____

What story really resonated with me?

_____

What was it about it that I liked?

_____

_____

What do I want to change in my life relating to this?

_____

_____

When do I want that change to start?

_____

_____

What impact will this change have on my life?

_____

_____

"What we can or cannot do, what we consider possible or impossible, is rarely a function of our true capability. It is more likely a function of our beliefs about who we are."
– Anthony Robbins

ACTION 9.

Point/Name/Theme

_____

What story really resonated with me?

_____

What was it about it that I liked?

_____

_____

What do I want to change in my life relating to this?

_____

_____

When do I want that change to start?

_____

_____

What impact will this change have on my life?

_____

_____

"Remember, happiness doesn't depend upon who you are or what you have; it depends solely upon what you think."
– Dale Carnegie

ACTION 10.

Point/Name/Theme

_____

What story really resonated with me?

_____

What was it about it that I liked?

_____

_____

What do I want to change in my life relating to this?

_____

_____

When do I want that change to start?

_____

_____

What impact will this change have on my life?

_____

_____

"People are just as happy as they make up their minds to be."
– Abraham Lincoln

CONNECT WITH JOHN ON –

Linkedin – linkedin.com/in/johndabrowski

Twitter – @jdmindcoach

Facebook – facebook.com/jdmindcoach

Website – www.jdmindcoach.co.uk

Instagram – instagram.com/jdmindcoach

AND …

Email – john@jdmindcoach.co.uk

Telephone – 01159 713344